TRANSfORMATIVE
Meditation

ABOUT THE AUTHOR

Gayle Clayton is the founder of the Amarjah Center, an esoteric school for transforming and evolving consciousness. She earned a master's degree in religion, with a major in Buddhist philosophy. Having apprenticed with two modern masters, Gayle teaches introductory and advanced meditation workshops in the wisdom school tradition, and is a core faculty member of the Omega Institute of Holistic Studies.

TO WRITE TO THE AUTHOR

If you wish to contact the author or would like more information about this book, please write to the author in care of Llewellyn Worldwide and we will forward your request. Both the author and publisher appreciate hearing from you and learning of your enjoyment of this book and how it has helped you. Llewellyn Worldwide cannot guarantee that every letter written to the author can be answered, but all will be forwarded. Please write to:

Gayle Clayton
℅ Llewellyn Worldwide
P.O. Box 64383, Dept. 0-7387-0502-0
St. Paul, MN 55164-0383, U.S.A.
Please enclose a self-addressed stamped envelope for reply,
or $1.00 to cover costs. If outside U.S.A., enclose
international postal reply coupon.

Many of Llewellyn's authors have websites with additional information and resources. For more information, please visit our website at http://www.llewellyn.com.

TRANSFORMATIVE
Meditation

Personal & Group Practice to
Access Realms of Consciousness

GAYLE CLAYTON

2004
Llewellyn Publications
St. Paul, Minnesota 55164-0383, U.S.A.

First Edition
First Printing, 2004

Book design and editing by Karin Simoneau
Cover design and interior illustrations by Gavin Dayton Duffy
Cover image © Digital Vision, © Brand X, © Photodisc, & © Comstock

Library of Congress Cataloging-in-Publication Data
Clayton, Gayle, 1957–
    Transformative meditation: personal & group practice to access
    realms of consciousness / Gayle Clayton.
        p. cm.
    Includes bibliographical references and index.
    ISBN 0-7387-0502-0
        1. Meditation. 2. New Age movement. 3. Altered states of consciousness.
        4. Small groups—Religious aspects. I. Title.

BP605.N48C56 2004
204'.35—dc22   2003065909

Llewellyn Publications
A Division of Llewellyn Worldwide, Ltd.
P.O. Box 64383, Dept. 0-7387-0502-0
St. Paul, MN 55164-0383, U.S.A.
www.llewellyn.com

Printed in the United States of America

For Bryan, who opened my heart to a new world of possibilities.

Come, come, whoever you are
Wanderer, worshiper, lover of leaving
Ours is a caravan of eternal joy.
Even if you have broken your vows a hundred times,
Come, come, yet again come.

—Rumi

CONTENTS

ACKNOWLEDGMENTS

A very grateful thank you is extended to the many students and teachers who explored these exercises and relationships. My late teacher, Ron, inspired this foundation of work by reflecting the levels of consciousness through meditation, my personal path to the transcendent realms. Special thanks also to Dr. Shanta Ratnayaka, my major professor and teacher in Buddhist philosophy, and to Julie Wallace and Trish McCartney, who assisted me in expressing my ideas. Thank you to those who contributed in invaluable ways to this work: Dr. Christina Wright, Claire Lewis, Michelle Mather, LISW, and Rachel Bianco. *Namasté*.

INTRODUCTION

To paraphrase Margaret Mead, a small group of conscious committed people can change the world. As our mission statement for this meditation system for transformation, I find that it not only provides meaning for our spiritual work, but also creates a ray of hope as humanity evolves through an evermore complex world. Our technological advances must be balanced with the wisdom of the ages. In this ever-changing world, we constantly create, maintain, and then destroy to be reborn again. By choosing to be consciously involved within this cycle, highly aware groups prepare for the evolution of higher consciousness in our world.

In this meditative transformation system, you will learn to access, utilize, and maintain many different realms of consciousness. Each defined level has its own unique energetic principles with corresponding rules, gifts, and challenges. Some seekers acquire higher faculties such as clairvoyance, healing energies, foreknowledge, and innumerable visions and insightful teachings. However, for the true initiate, the only end goal is to simply know the truth. In the final analysis, the words written outside of the Oracle of Delphi's cave hold the greatest truth, "Know thyself." By mastering the entire spectrum of consciousness, you will find a mystical awareness—a unity that transcends space and time.

However, the work of transformation is not limited to just self; in mystical awareness, there is no other. All manifestation is a reflection of self. Within the Mahayana Buddhist tradition, the bodhisattva vow is to postpone enlightenment until all beings may achieve it. In the mystical sense, this vow may be understood as simply regaining wholeness by uniting the various aspects of self to become transcendent.

These fundamental principles of energy transformation within this meditation system have been sustained through the many civilizations that cultivated this planet. Small esoteric organizations and mystical branches of various religions maintained a wisdom tradition of evolving higher consciousness for personal and planetary development.

My first encounter with such a wisdom school was the result of my search for a spiritual teacher. The modern adaptation of a wisdom school, having less to do with the agricultural based ancient religions of the mystery schools, contained an eclectic blend of many religious traditions. At the same time, I selected a traditional Buddhist monk and professor for my graduate academic studies in religion. The wisdom school teachings were juxtaposed with the Theravada branch of Buddhism. Through the conflicting guidance of having two great teachers simultaneously, I eventually learned my truth by comparing and contrasting their vastly different perspectives to form my own.

In working with meditation groups for transformation, the comparison of experiences provides valuable perspectives. Consider the Sufi story of several blind men being led into a large room where an elephant munches his hay. The men are instructed to discover the essence or defining characteristics of the animal sharing their space. The first man, after stumbling around, bumps into the elephant's leg. Elated, he cried out, "An elephant is strong and round like a tree trunk." The second man, having found within his grasp the elephant's large, flopping ear, countered, "No, an elephant is just like a blanket. It is flat and wide." A third man, feeling the movement of the elephant's tail, grabbed it and countered with, "An elephant is more like a rope. See how it coils and moves." You who have eyes to see may understand at a different level that each blind man had captured an identifiable aspect of the elephant, but none had been able to grasp the totality of the elephant's being. Similarly, in the wisdom school tradition I learned various teachings and practices to realize that many different paths may lead to mystical awareness or unity consciousness.

The wisdom school tradition of teachings loosely weaves a tapestry of teachings from the world's mystical traditions, affording multiple perspectives of the mystical state. Generally, wisdom schools are headed by a single teacher who has attained mastery in the mystical realms. Seekers drawn to participate in these teachings explore many paths to the sacred; the subjects may include sacred geometry, meditation, music, poetry, and philosophy. After an introductory training session typically lasting one to two years, the candidates are evaluated for initiation.

Originally, the initiation into the wisdom school required ego completion, a state of wholeness where an individual is no longer motivated by unconscious internal desires. While still a necessary component to personal transformation, ego completion can be enhanced through group dynamics and direct experiences of higher realms of consciousness through a working group. The working group consists of dedicated students who, under the aware guidance of a teacher, act as a mirror to individual actions. In this way, the meditation working group provides the tools to uncondition self and unravel personal karmic knots. Conditioning that once taught you how to be a viable link in social structures may also prohibit your direct experience of true reality. A group allows you to combine strengths and overcome normal obstacles to the truth.

Throughout this book, I present refined, tested, and proven techniques to experience various realms of higher consciousness through the use of a working group. Each of these vibratory levels is separated by a membrane that the mystic cannot see, but it may prohibit seekers from feeling higher levels of awareness. As more groups explored this system of meditation, universal markers emerged at the entrance to each realm to determine progress and identify areas needing development.

In a recent newsletter, I published a painting I did over fifteen years ago. At the time, I had just quit a lucrative job with no firm plans for future direction, and I cried out in frustration to know what was driving me to change every aspect of my life. I painted furiously and, without knowing why, I attempted to paint the inside of my mind. Though the painting is primitive, the work had meaning. I wasn't sure what it meant, but I kept it over the years. Now, knowing the exploratory dynamics of higher consciousness, I realize that the painting depicted these identifying universal markers.

As my teaching evolved, I learned how to initiate others into these realms of higher awareness through meditation. Ultimately, human consciousness must expand and develop a different operating mode to connect with these higher spaces. This, by itself, is not such a unique discovery. Carlos Castaneda outlined a system of consciousness with his initiations with Don Juan. Ken Wilber, in a brilliant early work, outlined a psycho-spiritual spectrum of consciousness. Others have combined yoga, meditation, art, poetry, and consciousness. The unique feature to this system is the use of group or collective meditation to transform not just a single person, but groups of people. There is not just a room of individuals meditating, but there is a single identity made of separate members.

Finally, the meditation work of transformation reveals the mystical awareness of truth. By applying principles of meditation in conjunction with the combined energies of various group and individual practices, this meditation system transforms the individuals, the group, and, later, the world. Linked consciousness allows a group to focus with great clarity on personal and global spiritual work.

Within mystical awareness there is no separateness, but only a true identity that shares consciousness with all life. The human being is simply a microcosm of the macrocosm. To know thyself is to follow the inner wisdom in alignment with the ultimate truth to perform the work that is given to us to do. In knowing our true identity, we are guided step-by-step, moment-by-moment, and sustained and supported by the eternal universal forces. A matrix of pure energies and aware groups creates a new vision of the world; one that transcends egoic desires and strives for harmonious coexistence. While transformative meditation provides a rich, full awareness of being in your personal meditations, there is also a link to a greater spiritual work. We must learn to live in harmony with the planet, bring more mindfulness into our world, and transform the energies to create a conscious balance in all life. Our work in meditation is an invaluable tool for evolving higher consciousness.

Chapter One

MEDITATION: IT'S MORE THAN YOU THINK!

Mention meditation to casual friends and images of robed monks chanting "om" immediately come to mind. If you probe further into the memory banks, some people recall the transcendental meditation (TM) that was popularized during the free-flowing cultural awakenings of the 1960s. Today, however, meditation has been publicized as an effective practice to combat stress, heart disease, and anxiety. In our wellness focus, meditation along with massage therapy and yoga has become integrated among mainstream medical practices. Yet, even though meditation for relaxation is more accepted today, the exploration of meditation as a path to enlightenment and its hidden doorways into mysticism are yet to be explored by the majority of people. The mystical realms are left to those who are more than casual seekers.

What is meditation? Meditation, for many people, means a practice to achieve relaxation and a stillness of the mind. Early introductions to meditation begin with a teacher or tape inviting you to close your eyes and follow a story coaching you to relax. Other practices lead you on an imaginary journey to an inspired goal. Some practices entail focusing on the breath and learning to relax the body limb by limb, organ by organ. Both relaxation scripts and creative visualization are beneficial introductions for beginning individual and group meditations, and may migrate into deeper practices. Both share elemental considerations of environment, position, focus, and reflection.

The best way to learn meditation is to begin with a simple sitting. The following guidelines are suggestions on how to begin. Meditation is an inward journey and an exploration of self. Cultivate a willingness to explore and experiment. Through practice and a careful examination of your results, you can progress into higher realms of meditation. Results can be expedited and enhanced by working with a good teacher and/or a good meditation group, as will be discussed later.

INSTRUCTIONS FOR BEGINNING MEDITATION

Create a Favorable Environment

Meditation can be done anywhere at any time, but taking care to create a conducive environment greatly enhances a beginner's experience. First, select a place that can be dedicated at least temporarily to your practice. You may choose a favorite corner in your living room, an uncluttered closet floor in your guest bedroom, or even a comfortable but infrequently used chair in your dining room. A friend of mine uses a low shelf in her office to hold her sacred objects and keeps a firm meditation pillow behind her door. Dedicating a special place to meditation reminds you of your practice each time you encounter the spot.

Note also that the place where you practice regularly also begins to store the energy generated by your work. All matter is the interplay of energy at different vibrations, and meditation enhances the inherent levels. In addition to having their own natural vibration, the natural woods, carpet fibers, or quartz stone resonates to the frequencies generated by quieting the mind. Consider the sound of a babbling brook as it makes its way over the rocks in its path. Remove or add a rock and the sound of the stream changes. Sometimes higher notes emerge and at other times, the sounds may even disappear. Yet it takes the water, the shape of the ground, the forces of gravity, and objects in the path to create the babbling brook. Adding your conscious energy to any environment changes the frequency and interplay of energies.

In the world of energy and form, all vibratory fields overlap. As you practice meditation in the same place, the objects in your environment resonate with higher meditative energy. In a reciprocal manner, the sacred place you create for your practice may even assist you in finding the clarity and awareness you seek. The sacred objects remind you of your last meditation, and you are drawn into the memory of that space. In that mental realm where you remember and observe your last meditation, you are already beginning to meditate in the present. Your energy is raised by the higher patterns stored and maintained in your surroundings.

Eliminate as many worldly distractions as possible in your chosen meditation place. Take time to turn off the phone or to silence your answering machine. Stop the ticking of a pendulum or clock. Turn off the ceiling fan, as the drone of its motor may lull you to sleep. Choose a place where you cannot hear the television or computer games. These modern devices deliberately utilize patterns to attract your attention to them. Initially it is important to have a quiet, comfortable place to begin your practice. After your practice is firmly established, you may find that very little distracts you.

Note that distractions vary for different people. If you are habituated to the level of background activity in a small New York City apartment with blaring horns, sirens, traffic, and neighbors, you may find your needs are different from those in a remote West Virginia cabin. Experiment with creating your sacred environment and overcoming background distractions.

Since meditation work enhances the senses, you may wish to use soft lighting or even a special candle. Vision is often the primary choice to process reality. In beginning meditation, the instructions frequently request that the eyes be closed. At the end of the session, the eyes are more sensitive in the same way that you are upon first awakening. You may find that using low-wattage lamps, rope lighting, or candlelight prevents a glaring reentry into your sacred space.

Your meditation space may also include objects that have special meaning to you. Sometimes a prayer rug or a wall hanging can evoke a quiet, more sacred atmosphere. Statues of gods and goddesses whose qualities you wish to invoke, or a beautiful plant may be placed in your space. I recently walked into someone's home and in the entry was a beautiful jade statue of Kuan Yin, the goddess of compassion, prominently displayed on a marble table against a mirrored wall. Large white roses and budding tree branches framed her graceful standing form. Immediately, I found reverence and compassion reflected to me. Your space need not be so elaborate, but allow it to become a pleasant reflection of your inner divine nature.

Choose an appropriate time for your sitting in meditation. As human beings are creatures of habit, regular times enhance practice. Even now, I have an inner sense when it is 9 p.m., as I have been practicing meditation for years at that time. Friends and family have learned that I reserve this special time for me, and honor my privacy and practice. You should choose a time that is conducive for your life schedule. Consider carefully whether this will be before the children come home, early in the morning before the day's activities begin, or at midday when you take a break from work. Don't try the time just before you go to sleep, as that may sabotage your practice. In the relaxed meditative state, you may find it too easy to fall asleep. Finally, you may wish to set a gentle timer to remind you of the end of your time committed to meditation. Be sure to do so if you have to return to work or other worldly commitments, since you can easily lose track of time in meditation.

Find a Supportive Posture

Posture is extremely important for successful meditation. There are many Buddhist and yoga techniques from which to draw inspiration for exploration. I once attended a meditation sitting with a Tibetan monk in residence in Woodstock, New York, who included over three hours of instruction on proper posture. Yet, I know many very good practitioners who meditate in unsanctioned positions.

In the beginning, try a position that allows the spine to be naturally straight. Many people find that when sitting on the floor, a dense pillow or a more supportive buckwheat-filled cushion places the pelvis at a higher level than the feet and knees. This alignment inhibits the problem of your feet falling asleep. If you choose to sit on the floor, it is not necessary to assume the lotus position, which has the feet placed on the thighs. While that position offers advantages for some, your initial encounters of meditation should not be sidetracked by the constant pain of assuming what may not initially be a natural position for you. Experimentation with position will help you find the proper meditative posture for you. Some people begin by sitting in a straight-back chair with their feet flat on the floor. There are also specially designed meditation benches that coax your body into a balanced position. Whether you use these or not, observe your posture. Look for tension in the body, and see if the tilt of the head or a change in the resting place of the foot attain a more relaxed and balanced posture. Sometimes a mirror or a simple before-and-after photograph can reveal much about position.

Positions may evolve as your ability to sit quietly develops. Make sure that your meditation position allows your body to be in balance. There should be enough tension to keep it upright, but not enough as to cause strain in the body. Following are some checkpoints and suggestions to try with variations in your posture. You may only want to vary one element at a time so that the effect will be isolated. Over time you may want to come back to these suggestions to see if your responses have changed.

1. Make sure that you are sitting on your pelvic bones and your seat is not pushed forward. If you are used to slouching in your chair, this more upright position may at first feel unnatural and require some adjustment on your part. Lean forward or backward a little more than usual and see how that affects your posture.

2. Ensure that your head is balanced on the top of your spine. Feel the muscles around your neck and upper shoulder area. If you feel tense there, you may be using muscle tension instead of proper alignment to hold your head in position. Try moving your entire head back, but not tilted, and feel the difference in your muscles.

Try dropping the chin and see how that affects your posture. Sometimes people report an energetic rush through the body when they finally locate the proper position for them. For now, try very slowly rolling the head in a circle and observe how the muscles, skeleton, and neck respond.

3. Place your hands gently in a natural position in your lap. If you interlace your fingers with the left thumb over the right, try reversing them the next time and see how that feels. If your hands are not touching, but resting on your thighs, you may wish to place your hands on your knees. In your next sitting, you can experiment by placing the palms down on the knees instead of up. Explore if that makes a difference in how you feel or how your meditation progresses. Try forming a circle with your thumb and index finger on each hand. At another sitting, interlock those two circles. Perhaps you feel more comfortable by bringing the hands together in a prayer pose.

When I had suffered a debilitating back injury, I found that the only posture I could maintain was a prone position. Lying down and in great pain, I explored how subtle movements could shift my awareness. Through this changed practice, I also learned that a clearer mind and proper position alleviated the physical pain. While meditation can be done while lying down, the temptation to fall asleep greatly increases. Generally, the seated position is recommended.

In your own practice, you might also get ideas on posture through reading sacred texts, observing the postures in sacred statues, or holding specific hand positions, called *mudras,* and observing how adjusting your position subtly changes how your body feels. Exploration of posture will enhance your meditation abilities.

Establish a Meditative Focus

Left alone, our minds tend to drift aimlessly. Meditation is a practice that develops mastery over the wanderings of the mind. With time, you will find that regular practice produces a quiet, still mind and an inner peace. Through your sittings, you learn to focus and adjust the mind as it loses awareness and begins to daydream. In doing so, you are training the mind to be still. Each time it wanders, you bring it back to focus through observation. The objects of focus can include special breathing techniques, *mantras,* which are sounds or words to repeat, sacred art, called *mandalas,* candles, and even chants. One of the easiest mantras to begin with is the sound of your name. Say it repeatedly until you find yourself performing the mechanics without thinking.

When the mind is still, our awareness increases. There is a heightened awareness of all the senses, an intense clarity of an uncluttered mind, and an enhanced ability to concentrate. While in graduate school, I found that meditation enhanced my ability to recall information as well. When a challenging test question confronted me, I was able to meditate, remember the class lecture, and form a response from that information. A disciplined, focused mind offers many advantageous by-products in the process of transformation.

Already you have learned the first task in training the mind—simple observation. The emphasis on posture has provided a focus: to observe the current situation, make simple changes, observe the reaction, and adjust accordingly. As you establish a posture that works for you, or you simply adjust to the one you are in, you may expand your focus from the body to include its senses.

So often in our world it is difficult to find personal time to simply observe the data the physical body is sensing. In meditation, as we stop doing and simply notice, the mind naturally allows the senses to enter into awareness. Most practices of meditation begin by closing the eyes and focusing on the breath. Breath is life. While we can live for a short time without food or water, breath is an almost immediate need. Breath is one act that is greatly enhanced by bringing attention to it. Most of us have learned to be shallow breathers and seldom employ the full capacity of our lungs. Following are ways to expand the breath:

1. Take in a full, deep breath, and note how both the chest *and* the stomach expand.

2. As you exhale, note how the stomach and chest contract to force out all of the expended air.

3. Take a few deep breaths in succession while observing the body's rhythmic cycle of expansion and contraction, and note how you feel.

It's hard to hurry when you're breathing deeply. The focus on the breath brings a natural stilling of the body. The deep breathing allows more oxygen into your system and forces out the consumed air. With each breath you take in air, extract the nourishment from it, and then return it, changed, into the atmosphere. With every breath, you breathe in life, consume it, and then expel it. With every breath, the world is created, maintained, and destroyed. No wonder so many traditions begin meditation with the focus on breathing.

Closing the eyes provides an enhanced awareness of the other senses. With your eyes shut, notice how your hearing picks up the subtle background noises—the sound of someone walking by, the sound your breath makes as it passes in and out of your body, or the song of the birds singing outside of your space. But don't be distracted by these noises or allow your attention to be drawn and focused on them. Instead, stay focused on being aware within the body. The sounds simply exist, and are an integral part of your awareness. For example, the bird sings its song outside my window. The song is just a song. However, if I begin to wonder whether it is a mockingbird or not, I have allowed the bird's song to distract me. If the song is just there, but my mind is still open and clear, my meditation is going well. Now, in turn, notice the more subtle senses of taste, smell, and touch. Is there a lingering subtle taste of mouthwash? Does the fragrance in your laundry detergent remain noticeable in your clothes? How does the carpet, floor, or chair support your body? Notice the details that your body is providing you, yet allow that awareness to include the senses without being distracted.

Then, as the sensory data is merged into expanded awareness, the mind opens into the emotional realm. Frequently, unresolved emotional experiences arise—the argument with children over breakfast, your anxiety about your job performance review, or other unresolved concerns. If you become distracted and become lost in an emotional drama unfolding, simply begin again to observe the breath until you find clarity. In the clearer mind, you may once again expand your awareness to include the sensory input. Just notice how you are feeling. Are you feeling pleasant or unpleasant? Simply identify your emotional state with either of those terms. If the emotional issues come up, observe if they are pleasant or unpleasant, and let them rest in your mind quietly without entering into their drama.

Sometimes, however, the emotional realm is too difficult to allow the existence of charged issues without distraction. Even though I have practiced meditation for many years, there are times when I realize the issue isn't going to disappear. So, I accept that there are just some days that my meditation isn't going to be as high and clear as I desire. Consequently, I begin to use my meditation time to examine the troublesome issue. By observing the issue as if I were analyzing a movie or stage drama, I look at all the players that contribute to the conflict, the underlying issues, and my own patterns with resolving tension. In doing so, I gain perspective on the problem. If I can, I let the issue's dynamics exist within my awareness and continue to meditate. Otherwise, I simply sit with the issue. The focus and attention brought to any unresolved concern eventually results in unraveling emotional and mental attachments. When you are challenged in your meditation, you may try to continue to meditate, or simply hold the committed time and realize that you can try again tomorrow.

In a successful meditation sitting, where the emotional tensions subside, the mind once again finds a clear, quiet state, but this is often only a transitory occurrence, as a thought will almost immediately come into the mind. The undisciplined mind finds the simple clarity ripe to interject random thoughts such as, "Did I leave the stove on?" when you've just sat down, or, "I wonder what we're having for lunch?" Most of these thoughts are simply the mind chattering to fill its void. Nature abhors a vacuum. On the rare occasion, however, the thought is a valid reminder. You may want to stop meditation long enough to jot down the thought so you'll remember it later. Hopefully you will then be able to return to a clear mind, where the thoughts drift in and out of awareness, and eventually find a quiet mind. Until you do, let thoughts pass through you, knowing that you can pick them up at a later time.

Many people find transcending the thought process to be the most difficult phase in learning meditation. Persistence and practice will pay off by finding a place that is still, quiet, and devoid of thoughts. Ultimately, meditation practice leads the mind into a place that many call "emptiness." In this moment, the meditation becomes timeless and the body is in a blissful state. There is no tension in the body, the emotional realm, or in the world of thoughts. This is the goal of personal meditation—a place of stillness.

Reflect on Your Experience

As Plato stated: "An unexamined life is not worth living." As a learning tool, each meditation experience inspires a nonjudgmental reflective examination. You can learn from each sitting. The point of the examination is not to judge or compare your meditation, but to learn what does or does not work for you. For example, you may have found that in your last session your cat entered the room and began nuzzling you. If the cat distracted you, you learn to shut the door to exclude him or her from your meditation space the next time you sit. A gentle analysis after each session provides an opportunity to enhance the next.

Even a meditation session that leads you to a blissful stillness offers you learning opportunities. What factors contributed to your success? The change of posture, time of day, or state of mind may all influence your meditation. When you realize the content stillness that meditation provides, your practice is validated by the experience of a state of pure joy. When you feel this bliss, your practice becomes easy, your sitting timeless, and your perspective of life greatly enhanced. You have been successful. Now that you have found that state, you will recognize it more quickly the next time it happens. As in most skills, the more regularly you practice, the greater your achievement.

Before entering a meditation group, some people are more comfortable if they have had an opportunity to work alone or if they have some rudimentary knowledge of meditation. If you fall into this category, you can record the following script to play back, or have a good friend read it slowly to you. This exercise should take ten to fifteen minutes.

RELAXATION EXERCISE

Let's begin this relaxation exercise by finding a quiet, safe place to meditate. Turn off the television, phone, and any other distractions that might interrupt your session. Find a comfortable sitting position. It doesn't matter if it is on a chair or sitting cross-legged on a pillow on the floor. It's important that the body be comfortable without being so relaxed that it falls asleep. For most people, this means that you should be seated with your spine relatively straight and your feet flat on the floor. Sitting straight allows you to take full and deep breaths. If you are lying down, try putting a rolled towel or pillow under your knees. This helps you remain in position without allowing your body to turn into a sleeping position or create stress on your back or knees. Uncross your arms and let them extend naturally alongside your body. Allow yourself to take a couple of really deep breaths.

Now, I invite you to close your eyes. With the eyes closed, the focus turns from the outside world into our own internal self. Place your attention on making the next few breaths deeper and fuller. Notice how the chest as well as the belly expands when you fill your lungs completely. Your body responds by relaxing while your mind stays alert. Adjust your position as necessary so that you are not distracted by the discomfort of your body. Eventually you will find a position where your body balances naturally, the breath becomes deep and regular, and you are conscious and aware. This simple act of breathing correctly and fully naturally brings both the body and the mind into a state of relaxation.

After a few minutes, you will find that you are breathing deeply and regularly, much as you do when you fall asleep. In meditation, though, you want to keep the relaxed body state while maintaining an alert and conscious mind. You can easily hear the sound of these words while allowing yourself to breathe regularly. There's nothing to do and nowhere to go. If thoughts arise, promise to remember them later and return your focus to the breath. You may even keep a pad and pencil at your side to jot them down if the thoughts distract you too much. Explore ways to let the thoughts pass.

Note whether or not there is any tension in the body. Are your shoulders relaxed? If there is tightness in your neck, move your head slightly to find a place where it balances correctly on the top of your spine. Breathe fresh air into those areas, and exhale any tightness out of your body. Just breathe. Any time your mind wants to wander, just bring it to focus on deep breathing. That, indeed, is the discipline of meditation. Gently guide the mind to focus and the body to relax.

Breathe in a deep, full breath. Hold it just for a moment before you exhale through the mouth. Note how that changes the rhythm and feeling of breathing. Continue noticing the body as it sits or lies in a relaxed position. Unclench the fists and let the fingers extend. Let the belly be relaxed and full; there's no need to hold it clenched and tight. Let the chest expand fully and then completely release all of the air it holds. How is the small of your back? Breathe deeply and let it relax.

Continue breathing gently and fully. If you find these words distracting, just focus on your breathing and on relaxing any tension you discover in your body. There is nothing you can do wrong in this exercise. Trust your breath and your process of relaxing. These words are only suggestions or reminders to notice areas of your body that you may not normally pay attention to.

Continue to emphasize the breath, and keep the mind alert. If after practice you discover that you're falling asleep, you may change several factors to assist you with staying awake. Of course, if you're having trouble falling asleep, you might find this relaxation exercise extremely beneficial.

If you have difficulty staying awake, you may want to try meditating in the morning versus the evening, or try opening a window. You can also imagine that with each breath you are bringing fresh oxygen into your brain, enlivening and enriching it. With each breath, you refresh the brain by bringing in more oxygen and taking the processed carbon dioxide out of the body.

The breath is often equated with life. With every breath you take, you bring life into the cells of your body, nourishing it. With every exhalation, you expel that which you no longer need. The human breath is part of the cycle of life. Breathe. Breathe deeply.

Allow the tension of your legs to dissipate. If your limbs are falling asleep, adjust your position quietly and respectfully. Be gentle with your body—it is the expressive vehicle you possess. Let it relax and enjoy a few moments of relaxed silence.

After completion of this session, take a moment or two to notice how being still is felt within the body. Know that this peaceful feeling is available to you at any time by simply observing the breath. In many forms of meditation, this is comparable to finding your center, a place where you simply are—no masks, no filters, no pretending. If you find yourself being tense during your day, just take a moment to find this center. This is a simple practice that can be done anywhere at any time. Namasté. I honor the divine within you.

Use a bell or gentle timer to mark the end of meditation.

While this is an example of a basic meditation technique, you will find many variations on this theme. Some instructors may spend more time describing each muscle and allowing it to relax before going on to the next muscle. In doing so, you become much more aware of your body and position in a positive sense.

The physical body provides feedback as well. Generally, I can determine a person's clarity by the level of relaxation in the face. When working closely with students, I often take a digital photo of them before meditation. Then, after we have gone through the relaxation exercise, I snap another photo for comparison. Most are amazed that there initially is so much tension in their face. The masks of fixed smiles, or worried, furrowed brows take a lot of energy to maintain. When you become centered and relaxed, the patterned expressions on your face relax into a peaceful, soft expression. I remind serious students gently and frequently to simply relax their face. It's hard to maintain anger with a soft face, as well as to maintain the masks that hide true identity. As the true identity is unveiled, the radiant inner beauty shines through. The relaxation meditation technique takes its name from its goal, and almost everyone can benefit from this simple exercise.

On the other hand, in creative visualization the instructor leads you on a journey and allows you, with a simple suggestion, to fill in gaps with images from your own consciousness. The process of creative visualization became national news when Jean Houston coached Hillary Clinton to visualize a public figure from whom she could learn grace under conflict. Hillary's session with the imaginary Eleanor Roosevelt created a national backlash through media exploitation. Most people, however, find that creative visualization is easy to do and categorize the practice along the lines of daydreaming with a purpose. If the imagery is not working for you, dare to explore where your mind leads you during an exercise. Just remember that there are subtle messages for you that arise from your subconscious, or perhaps messages from your higher self descend into your awareness. Visualization is a gentle introduction to meditation; children especially enjoy these interactive stories.

GUIDED VISUALIZATION EXERCISES

Exercise 1

Find a comfortable position for this fifteen- to twenty-minute exercise. Make sure that there won't be any distractions such as the phone, television, or visitors. Dim the lights, get comfortable, and let's begin a personal journey of discovery.

Close your eyes and relax for a few moments. Now, imagine that you are seated in your comfortable chair at your favorite location. Where are you? Look around. Are you there by yourself or are their others around you? Relax, as you are totally in control of this experience. What do you notice about your surroundings? [Pause.] What are you wearing? [Pause.]

Now imagine that an animal appears magically in front of you. You are grateful and pleased at this sudden turn of events. Now you can share telepathically with this wise being the qualities that you have been seeking internally. Deep empathetic eyes listen as you reveal your questions and issues. A kind response is telepathically transmitted to you. You allow this information to slowly find its place in your memory.

You find yourself willing to open your heart to your new friend. While the sharing has already alleviated your tension, the experience is not over. The wise animal reaches for something to give you. You receive a small gift that you can use to access your own inner wisdom. You examine it with awe. What is its purpose or message? Listen to it. Be open. You hold it in your open palm and marvel at how it eases your worries. This gentle reminder can be taken back with you as you return from this journey. Whenever you think of it, or even see a picture of a similar item, you will remember your own personal wisdom and find easy access to resolve the issues facing you. Take a moment to breathe deeply. When you are ready, open your eyes.

Exercise 2

Make yourself comfortable as we take an imaginary journey together. Let's begin by imagining you are in a forest. What kind of trees surround you? Are they old trees or is this a relatively new forest? Are there leaves on the trees or are they bare? Look around you. Is there light filtering through the canopy? Now, as you look around, you notice that there is a path that leads through the trees. Is it well worn?

Is it made in the dirt or is it paved with stones or brick? What does the terrain look like? Let your imagination fill in the picture for you.

Notice that as the path bends, there is water in front of you. Is it a large pool or a running creek? Pause for a moment on your journey. Listen to all the sounds around you. Are there animals in the forest with you? Is the wind blowing through the trees? Take a moment to notice your reflection in the pool of water. What do you look like?

As you prepare to leave the water, you notice that the path continues up a little hill. You climb with ease and grace. Yet as you near the crest, you notice that there is a fence obstructing the path. Describe the fence in detail.

Since you know the path must continue on the other side, how do you plan to get there? Look about you. Be creative. Know that your imagination holds the perfect answer for you. Go boldly to continue your journey. Once you make it over the fence, look around you and describe the new scenery.

When you are done, take a deep breath, and allow your eyes to open and focus again on being fully present in the moment.

This particular exercise employs many universal elements. For example, the description of the forest indicates a person's impression of his or her current life situation. Are the trees old and wise, or new growth after a forest fire? Your version of the path suggests how an individual traverses through life. Are you making it an uphill battle or is it an easy-coasting downhill? Your encounter with the size and scope of the water may provide an indication of how you allow love in your life. Is it an immense pool that you draw from, or is it a small stream trickling away from you? Your reflection in the water provides an opportunity to see how you view yourself. Are your eyes calm and your face relaxed, or is your face worried and tired? The fence indicates how you overcome obstacles in your path. Notice if you chose traditional or nontraditional methods, such as flying, to clear the fence. Once the obstacles are overcome, in the new scenery you will see how you are being rewarded. You may be amused to find that I once did this exercise with my sales applicants to determine which ones I should hire.

Visualization serves many students well, as it provides enough structure for them to relax and open to the world of higher perception. At the same time, careful wording in the second visualization reveals a great deal about people—how they see themselves, how they strive to overcome obstacles, and what they dream. Whether from the subconscious or the higher consciousness, these potent symbols reveal meaning to the beginning meditator.

Many practitioners combine relaxation and visualization. In hospitals or in medical treatments, healing imagery directs the mind's attention. My friend, Carolyn, was diagnosed with extremely large fibroid uterine tumors. The doctor informed her that surgery would be required if the tumors became larger. Carolyn, opting to avoid surgery, sought out alternative practices. She began visualizing an internal laser that kept zapping at the tumors, slowly chipping them away. Within eight weeks, Carolyn returned to the doctor, and her examination revealed no tumors whatsoever. Never underestimate the power of the body-mind connection.

Both visualization and relaxation are excellent practices, but neither completely fits the esoteric definition of meditation as spiritual introspection. As some people lightheartedly say, "Prayer is talking to God, while meditation is listening." In some ways, this could be true. Many prayers are based on personal desires and assistance in achieving desired outcomes. The importance of listening and being willing to consider the greater good in all situations are both aspects of meditation. While some serious meditation teachers disparage visualizations, they serve to focus diverse new groups. If the speaker's voice is imbued with higher awareness and the knowledge of mystical realms, the results are significant in sharing a high degree of consciousness.

The esoteric practice of meditation, however, leads to an empty, still experience of contemplation, and, if the quest is dedicated enough, to a mystical state. The mystical state is a union with ultimate divine reality. Meditators express a deep sense of unity and an enhanced way of being that typically defies rational expression. Many people express a transcendence of ego, a loss of time and space references, and an experience of great sacredness. The mystical state is frequently transitory, but engraved deep within consciousness as a peak moment in existence.

To further clarify terms, "meditation" and "contemplation" are not interchangeable, but have subtle distinctions. Meditation is the act or process of training the mind to experience higher awareness, while contemplation is the experience of being. The practice of meditation may employ techniques of counting the breaths as a means to focus the mind upon the bodily process. This focus may produce a trance-like rhythmic breathing or may simply engage the intellect. If you are thinking about the process, the experience of meditation is thwarted. Meditation is not a thinking exercise. Contemplation is a blissful experience of being fully aware within the real world.

While varying the meditation techniques of observing the breath and the environment produce different meditations, they seldom result in the state of contemplation. The meditative exercise should not be confused with the desired result of contemplation. Generally, being quiet and introspective will allow for the observance of things not normally noticed. Indeed, this is one way to begin the real work of meditation—becoming aware of things normally ignored. In order to achieve contemplation, you must learn through meditation to release conditioned responses that prevent your total awareness.

Conditioned responses are the methods you have learned to discriminate your attention. For example, as you read, you may be ignoring the television sound in the background or the sound of the dishwasher running. In order to concentrate on written thoughts, you have learned to tune out certain sensory awareness and focus on others. While this is useful while reading, filtering awareness also eliminates more subtle elements from your consciousness that you may not even realize you are missing. The practice of meditation expands your consciousness by releasing conditioned responses to allow the mind to become aware on many different levels.

Conditioning is a necessary process during human maturation, but one that you may choose to transcend as you mature. Babies are taught how to get what they need by observing their parents' responses. Indeed, through their experiences, children learn which acts produce desirable or undesirable responses. A complete operating system is established in order for a child to survive. Through the development of an ego, a child learns to ignore certain things and to pay attention to others. These patterns individualize a child and can operate throughout a lifetime.

Sometimes personal growth experiences such as a divorce or a spiritual crisis require a person to update his or her patterns. However, many people wander through life allowing these patterns of childhood experiences to unconsciously rule their life. They are asleep to their real motivations and goals. The spiritual seeker ultimately releases all conditioning in order to find his or her inner essence or true identity. The true identity reveals a person who is fully aware of all realms of awareness and faces the world with openness, vulnerability, and truth. Many schools of enlightenment refer to people who live unaware of their true nature as being "asleep." When awakened from darkness, they are considered enlightened. The process of becoming enlightened is difficult. A person must explore the darkness of the unknown self in order to find the inner light of the transcendent identity. Individuals must undergo careful self-examination using whatever tools, experiences, and teachers they can find. For many, meditation is a very effective personal tool of unraveling conditioned responses and masks to their true nature.

Can meditation and transformation be learned from a book? While meditation practices can be understood simply from reading a book, it is the practice that provides the learning and insight leading to enlightenment. Many books are written and read, but few people manage to transition the reading into the doing. For the exceptional person who accomplishes the latter, the written explanation may be enough for him or her to self-initiate into the higher realms of consciousness. At the same time, most people need guidance to look beyond their own conditioning and peer support to continue the quest. In many cases, sitting with an enlightened teacher may change the experience of meditation completely. Yet, a book remains a valuable resource for the serious meditation student, as well as a competent guide for establishing a foundation of knowledge upon which to build.

A trained teacher initiates an aspirant into realms that the student has never recognized. I personally sat with many self-proclaimed teachers until I met a true teacher. When I asked a question of this man, a brilliant golden light transformed the room until I was only aware of his dark eyes gazing into the depths of my soul. While there was no degree to support this teacher, no formal tradition, nor any tangible proof as to his mastery, he was able to reflect my experiences of higher realms of consciousness. My first session with him established an entangled relationship of personal growth and revelation. When you are ready, the right teacher and the appropriate teachings appear.

Until you find someone with whom to establish a working relationship, read books to gain background in the practice. Don't confuse intellectual knowledge with the experience. Let go of the expectations of a teacher and how you should relate. Participate in spiritual activities within your community. Networking frequently brings you into contact with a diverse group of people who may introduce you to their teacher. Fortunately, you may not have to trek to remote mountaintops to commune with a guru. Sit with an open mind and heart, and you will be rewarded with an appropriate teacher.

My teacher often said that I could learn as much from a bad teacher as I could from a good one. Recently, when I went to a seminar to see a nationally recognized speaker, the speaker stated emphatically that no one would ever be able to reach her level of expertise. Realizing that I could learn little from such a philosophy, I waited for a break, then left inconspicuously. Meanwhile, I examined how she answered questions from her large audience. I carefully noted which mannerisms engaged her audience and which did not. Though I no longer was interested in the speaker's lecture material, my own teaching repertoire now excludes and includes certain mannerisms and techniques that I learned from that long afternoon workshop. In your journey, continue to seek and question. A good teacher is not threatened by your inquiries. No matter how your journey begins, know that it is a continuing process of change.

The quest to enlightenment is difficult. Self-examination, doubt, and desire interweave in your journey to truth. Seekers most often inquire about their mission in life. No person can give another a reason to live. Frequently the goal is too large for seekers to understand all at once anyway, and could intimidate them on the journey. Truly, as you are ready, each step will reveal another level of your purpose. Be patient with yourself and your progress. Engage with other seekers to share and ground your experiences into reality. In a working meditation group, each person presents a different expression of the same event and proceeds at his or her own pace.

Finally, when you have found your truth, attempt to share it with others. Their reflections will assist you in refining your presentation and clarifying your own understanding. On the other hand, if your truth cannot withstand the questions raised by serious seekers, you may discover that you have not reached the highest understanding. There is ultimately only the truth, and it passes all questions.

Don't become discouraged. After the Buddha became enlightened, he hurried to share his realization with his small circle of peers. When he realized that he could not bring them into his understanding, the Buddha went into seclusion to explore ways to teach them. From that body of teachings arises many useful parables, benevolent guidelines for life, and techniques to achieve the enlightened mind. Your efforts will not only provide growth in understanding, but will also assist others who seek your wisdom.

MEDITATION IN A WORKING GROUP

Meditation is frequently thought of as a discipline, but since common usage leaves little distinction between it and contemplation, the term here will also mean "a way of being." Similar to any path of accomplishment, to achieve meditation as being, you frequently are required to spend years in the discipline aspect. Individuals may find clarity, health, peace, and many insights as rewards for participation that alone validate it as a worthwhile process. Yet there is a method of meditation that may provide assistance and expedite the process for the learning meditator. By consciously combining individuals into a single group, an individual's weaknesses may be countered by other individuals' strengths. By becoming a functional part of a working meditation group, members may experience new levels of awareness unavailable to them individually. Further, as the group progresses, so does the individual. Consider the group as a huge ship moving through a lock into the ocean of consciousness. Someone at the bow who passes through the lock first obtains recognition of the higher awareness, but as the ship continues its journey, everyone on board must pass through the gate. The group acts as a single meditating body. Eventually this type of group work leads all of its members into mystical awareness.

When the working meditation group progresses to a transpersonal awareness, the group shapes the forces evolving consciousness in this consensual reality. To accomplish this, there have been groups working throughout time to evolve consciousness. These groups developed meditation tools and markers to assist humanity in finding a more enlightened state. By training others in their transformation methods, these groups created a wisdom school, where a lineage of esoteric knowledge and process is transferred throughout time.

The wisdom school process transforms an individual into an enlightened being. The word "enlighten" has many different meanings; etymologically, it means "to illumine." The archaic meaning is derived from spiritual initiates' discovery of their inner light or wisdom. Enlightenment should not be confused with its gifts: clairvoyance, healing abilities, prophecy, and even magic. True enlightenment is a multifaceted understanding of the ultimate questions of life: why are we here and what is our purpose? A serious seeker will settle for nothing less than that truth.

Wisdom schools often introduce alternative states of being. The modern school uses meditation, not mind-altering drugs, to uncover higher realms. As this understanding integrates into our collective consciousness, our interactions within the world also change.

ADVENTURES WITH REALITY

A Ph.D. candidate wanted to know who I was. "Are you sure?" I asked. Evidently my answer intrigued him, and he persisted. Late one night we meditated together. Steve was tired, and his lowered resistance increased his potential to feel the transforming energies most people are conditioned to ignore. Suddenly, he sat up, alert and conscious.

"What happened?" I asked. Steve seemed unable to explain, so I said, "I'll tell you what happened to me and that might help. As we looked at each other, your face distorted, and then you morphed into other people. There were streaks of light in the room, and I could not see anything except you."

"When I looked at your face, you changed into different people," Steve replied. "At first this was fun and exciting, but then you turned into my best friend's mother." He was shocked.

These types of shocks to normal perception frequently hook people into beginning the wisdom school process. Awareness of a reality beyond "normal" creates an intensely personal mystery to explore. To resolve this experience, seekers learn to expand their personal under-standing of reality, thereby initiating an irreversible spiritual quest.

OBSTACLES AND ALLIES IN THE WISDOM SCHOOL

Modern wisdom school members are willing to explore themselves and their place in the universe. The ongoing student/teacher relationship provides the foundation of the work by illuminating obstacles on the spiritual path. A common barrier to truth is the self-imposed limitations of personality and ego. By uncovering layers of conditioning, the teacher assists in restructuring the ego into a complete and whole state. Only then may the ego be transcended and the inner essence revealed.

Most individuals find that cultural, educational, and parental conditioning limit their perception. A working meditation group assists the initiate in identifying unnecessary ego structures, attachments, and belief systems. Only then may the perception of truth be achieved.

THE ULTIMATE AIM

With the understanding of reality as it is, the wisdom schools teach how to consciously create soul. Then the individual consciousness and its experiences remain after the death of the physical body. The created soul holds purpose from lifetime to lifetime. With the knowledge of the soul, the initiate finds deeper meaning within daily activities. The "fixed" soul relates all actions, relationships, and events to a greater purpose; the student knows true identity.

BEYOND INDIVIDUAL ENLIGHTENMENT TO GROUP WORK

Initially the wisdom school involves individual work; however, many graduates join a working spiritual group comprised of enlightened members. A working group spends time, energy, and effort to achieve common goals that range from creating tools that enrich the group and society to preserving nature and exploring the cosmos. A working group serves not only its members, but also the world.

Properly formed, a working group creates a single consciousness that is far greater than any individual. Cultivating a team from different ethnic, cultural, and religious traditions, the group crosses boundaries to find fundamental truths. Eventually the group forms a single body with more clarity and insight than any of the individuals. The whole truly becomes greater than the sum of its parts.

A wisdom group draws archetypal or universal patterns of energies into a single collective mind; this model creates patterns of transforming energies within the world. While this work may challenge some belief systems, benevolent actions to enhance consciousness have always been a part of our civilizations. The inner workings of this spiritual group are beyond intellectual description; truly, the mysteries may only be experienced.[1]

From the wisdom school meditation techniques, a transformation of mind, body, and spirit evolves. Meditation within a group allows for the collective transcendence of personal boundaries, ego, and intellect. Personal transformation work not only has to be done, but is done within a group that serves to reflect the process in a supportive manner. Each member contributes to the process of the group that eventually forms a single body with more clarity and insight than any individual. While meditation is an experiential process, this book introduces guidelines for establishing working transformative meditation groups in the wisdom school tradition.

---

1. www.amarjah.org, Gayle Clayton, 2002.

Chapter Two

CONSCIOUSNESS & MYSTICISM

"When we know we are aware of something, we are conscious of it."

—Robert Ornstein

The study of meditation must include consciousness, a concept that can be difficult to define. However, most scientific and psychological experts can agree to three distinct categories of consciousness: sleep, the ordinary waking state, and the higher, more subtle levels of reality. Most people believe they understand waking reality; however, most people are conditioned to ignore many aspects of reality. The movie The Matrix addresses the issue of people being asleep to true reality. There is more going on than most people perceive. When the enhanced faculties of higher consciousness arise, you find the rich fullness of true reality.

How do you learn about realms of consciousness that you may have just recently discovered existed? In a working relationship, a teacher can introduce these enhanced levels of awareness through meditation, energy transmission, or by applying shocks to the psyche. These introductions open a world of possibilities for the spiritual seeker.

Even without the guidance of a teacher the psyche can shift with dramatic changes in your life. For example, when you experience the birth of a child your whole world opens up in unforeseen ways. Qualities and feelings that long lay dormant open with the modification of your life. You wonder and marvel at the complete dependency of this new life on you. Fortunately, most people rapidly assume the enhanced responsibility of parenthood. Life begins to operate at new levels of activity, awareness, and commitment. Each dramatic change in your life brings new opportunities for growth and the awakening of dormant abilities.

When working alone, you must find ways to create new experiences and relate them to something you already know. Frequently, these fleeting transcendent moments appear as a foreknowledge of events, experiencing something out of the ordinary, or unusually vivid dreams. The average person is conditioned to dismiss them without some method to establish their value in the mundane world. The value of an enlightened teacher is to reflect these subtle introductions to higher realms as well as provide guidance and feedback.

For most people, the process of learning is done by comparing and contrasting unknown events with known ones. I read of Carlos Castaneda's experiences as entertaining fiction until I began to have my own paranormal events. I reread his works during my own learning process to glean clues and clarity on how to understand and integrate these experiences. Though my own initiations did not include drugs, I found comfort in knowing that someone else had experienced similar visionary realms. I could identify with his fears and concerns. Castaneda's writings also secured my sanity by providing proof of these visionary realms. I could also compare my strange metaphysical events and attempt to implement the appropriate advice of his teacher. Additionally, since my own teacher had read Castaneda's works, we had a common vocabulary with which to relate hard-to-express ideas of different realms of consciousness that led to mystical awareness.

A mystical experience is a conscious encounter with total reality. Reality exists and can be perceived on many different levels, and is incomplete if only viewed from normal consciousness. Mystical experiences happen all the time, but conditioning screens them out of memory. While mystical events occur frequently in life, if they are not noticed, they disappear from your consciousness and memory.

These fleeting glimpses of the totality of reality contain signals, noises, thoughts, and other input that your consciousness has learned to ignore. In order to experience true reality on a continuous basis, you must undo the conditioning that prevents you from being totally aware.

For example, as you read this, notice again your environment, and particularly how habituated you are to your surroundings. You can easily tune out the clock, the television, or street noises. By screening out sensory or other input, the mind's capacity is reserved for work that is more complex. Yet, the work of an initiate is to undo this type of screening, and learn to expand the mind to holistically assimilate all levels of reality simultaneously. This requires a large increase in your capacity for consciousness, and meditation is one tool you can use to accomplish that goal.

First, however, there are some precautions to consider regarding conditioning. Certain automatic processes of the body should be allowed to remain subconscious. Breathing, digestion, heart rate, and so on are best left to a healthy body. There are other more mundane processes that may serve you well, so you may want to keep them as a subconscious response. For example, typing is a useful tool for me, since I have created a subconscious pattern to handle the details of typing. I automated, by practice, the act of typing words; otherwise, the process would require being conscious of every letter in every word, where that letter was located on the keyboard, and how hard to strike the requisite key to get the correct keyboard response. Also, typing is made more complex by actively coordinating the responding fingers, holding memory of what is to be typed, using the eyes to check typing, and filtering unrelated noises. If conscious of all these complex processes, I probably would not have enough capacity to think. For this reason, I created shortcuts by imprinting a series of individual acts into a simple neural pattern. My mind generates the appropriate physical actions of typing a word when I recognize it. My mental processing is freed from the bombardment of multiple sensory impulses and is available for more complex tasks.

There are also disadvantages to undoing conditioning and patterns. In the typing example, the combining of individual acts to create a single neural process is similar to a habit. Habits feature patterns for which certain stimuli generate specific responses. You may find that the fizz sound of pouring a soda makes you feel thirsty. As an initiate, you decide whether or not this habituation is productive for you. To break a bad habit, you must become conscious of both the stimulus and the expected response. Then you can choose whether or not to perform the act. New habits and shortcuts are useful tools to be used consciously, while their unconscious development may hinder a mystical perspective of reality.

Almost everyone has a mystical experience that provides a heightened awareness to life. William James writes in his book *Varieties of Mystical Experiences*[1] that there are four commonly accepted attributes to a mystical experience:

1. Heightened intellectual discernment.

2. Ineffability—the experiences are not easily verbalized.

3. Transience—the recognition and experience of these events is short-lived.

4. Divinity—Many attribute these experiences to a divine force higher than the individual.

The mystical experience produces a high state of intellectual clarity as a by-product. The mind assimilates facts, events, and people in a novel way that reveals a sudden insight or wisdom extending beyond that of rational logic. Often as an engineer, I assembled design criteria, manufacturing procedure, and customer feedback in a factual manner. In one instance, when I was unable to finalize the correct design to move forward, I put the problem aside. Later, when I was not even thinking about the product to be made, a solution popped to mind. Intuitively,

---

1. William James, *Varieties of Mystical Experiences* (New York: Scribner, Simon & Shuster, 1997).

I knew this was the right product design to go forward with, but I used my discerning intellect to back up my decision with logic. My mind had been processing this information in a realm above my daily awareness, and when it had found a solution, it brought that solution to my attention.

Mystical experiences are difficult to express. Some people use art, metaphor, or poetry, but no single expression addresses the subtleties of the experience appropriately. In the example of deciding on a product design, I could not relate to my team the decision process I had undergone. Being trained in sales, which is a form of conditioning that deals with meeting people's expectations, I provided my team with the factual information they needed, and I presented the information in a way that was easy for them to understand.

Conditioning can serve useful purposes. By sharing new ideas and goals in familiar terms and ways, people can more readily accept a change in direction. Perhaps this is the same motivation for different religions; the same truth is being presented through different cultural filters in an attempt to shift groups into a new perception. The diversity of expression enables the acceptance of new ideas, especially since the absolute truth defies quantification. This same concept is perhaps better expressed in the *Tao-Te Ching* as, "That which can be named is not the Tao." Expressions are filtered versions of the singular truth.

Mystical experiences are fleeting, yet when you are immersed in them you feel an enriched awareness and detail of that timeless moment. Recall a vivid moment in your life: perhaps it was your first kiss or the birth of a loved one. In that memory, you may find rich details such as the scent of flowers, the color of your clothing, or the rare feeling of complete intimacy. The encounter of a higher awareness that is stored in consciousness provides incredible detail that is frequently forgotten or replaced with other memories. A remembered mystical moment contains such fresh detail that it seems as if you are reliving the experience. These mystical moments are magical in quality and produce great meaning and purpose for living. During these moments and in the remembrance of them, there is a desire to always stay in that level of awareness. Life, in its fullest expression of consciousness, is a joy to live.

Finally, in mystical experiences there is a transcendence of the ego. There is no personal quality associated with the incident. Since the mystical event is difficult to describe or relate to others' experiences, most people consider such mystical experiences as grace bestowed by the divine. Grace is granted to an individual without necessarily being the result of any intent upon the behalf of the individual. Since this transcendent state is beyond the known realm of the ego, many people express it as an encounter with the sacred or holy. Whether the concept of divinity is a product of conditioning or inherent to an individual is an interesting aspect to contemplate.

While the mystical experience, until now, has been left to esoteric treatments and studies, it is becoming a new research frontier in modern psychology, medicine, and science. The University of Arizona at Tucson offers a graduate program in consciousness studies. Their program strives to establish scientific principles in the study of consciousness utilizing measurements, tests, and statistical information. The medical community is also exploring the body-mind link in ways to promote health and healing. Being a spiritual initiate, your experiences in mysticism involve even more responsibility and preparation. You must prepare body, mind, and spirit for an encounter with the laws of universal order found in the mystical realm. Through meditation or any system that utilizes energy transformation, you may find a path to becoming functional in higher realms of awareness.

FUNCTIONS OF CONSCIOUSNESS

The accomplishment of being conscious in higher levels rewards you with more awareness, but also more clarity in your life. As you become more conscious and functional, there are basic tools in each realm that you factor into your life decisions. More than just data, there are enhanced human faculties at work as well. You may find long-hidden talents such as clairvoyance, telepathy, or conversing with animals to aid you. The world of what others call "paranormal" becomes a part of your everyday world.

With wisdom, proper initiation, and a great deal of self-development work, a spiritual initiate may become a functional mystic. A functional mystic consciously selects specific realms to interact with and respond to appropriately. Imagine the kind of being who is able to function at realms beyond normal human functioning. You might call this person a priest, a magician, or a goddess. A functional mystic is someone who can operate in full realization of the ultimate truths while remaining fully functional in the mundane world. While there are a few such fully realized human beings, you will find that they live quiet lives of shared contemplation.

To join the ranks of functional mystics requires the integration of the entire spectrum of consciousness where you understand and perform the main functions of transforming energy at each level. Only then may you bring the highest energies into the lower realms to vitalize and catalyze groups. In the past, some secret societies in a bottoms-up scenario promoted the use of sacrificial offerings in order to transform enough energy to gain access to higher realms. Other groups used secret signals, combined sexual energies, and special astrological alignments to gain power outside the inherent humanness. While you may classify these acts as primitive, there are still groups using them today in attempts to gain power over events beyond personal control. No wonder there is such secrecy on the part of some esoteric societies. For the more sophisticated modern seeker, there are other systems that are used to understand the psycho-spiritual universe and access more energy than most can imagine and absorb.

There are as many paths to enlightenment as there are seekers. Many understand the world and their place in it through science. Facts, figures, and data support the intellect even as the initiate begins to transcend it. Modern seekers may find the quantum universe as a reflective tool for philosophic contemplation. Some seekers will search for the elusive religious teacher or spiritual guru who may hold their key for understanding through grace. Still others may explore psychotropic drugs or employ deprivation of sleep, food, or focus to achieve out-of-the-ordinary experiences. None of these extreme methods are recommended to access what, in the final analysis, is an inherently available tool. These extraordinary mystical experiences are accessible to most of humanity through the exploration of the mind. For many seekers and groups, meditation has proven to be an effective course for the study of higher consciousness.

In the higher uses of transformative meditation, conscious groups hold checks and balances in lower realms by applying energy in transforming existing world patterns of consciousness. Evolving consciousness has been the esoteric goal of many secret societies and ancient wisdom schools. According to Sufi psychologist Robert Ornstein, consciousness performs four major tasks:

1. Simplifying and selecting of information.

2. Guiding and overseeing actions.

3. Setting priorities for action.

4. Detecting and resolving discrepancies.

Any individual or group of individuals who share the ability to transform consciousness has the ability to exert certain controls over the mundane world. For the spiritual seeker, it is not the power that is the final goal; it is the wisdom to provide the harmonious relationships within a closed world system. The ethics, wisdom, and power to change the world also require a karmic responsibility to remain in the world that is being changed. As the saying goes, "Be careful of what you ask for; you might get it."

The shaping of the world in which we live is the subject of many fine books and well-developed movie plots. Certainly, the fear of being controlled by unseen forces resides in the American culture. Knowledge is frequently the antidote for fear; it is important to consider how consciousness creates reality.

SIMPLIFYING AND SELECTING INFORMATION

The first major function of consciousness is to simplify and select information. You might compare the process of tuning out information to the function of a computer monitor's screen saver. The original purpose of the screen saver was to prevent permanent burnout damage to expensive monitors, which was caused by leaving an unchanging display on the screen. A computer scans the monitor to see if any change has occurred since the last time the projection was monitored. If no changes are made after a period of time, the computer either shuts down the input to the monitor or activates a program that provides changing input to prevent burnout. Likewise, if your mind doesn't sense danger in the environment, it goes into an energy-saving pattern and monitors only changes in your surroundings and your focus.

In addition to the mind's "screen saver" ability, there is a wake-up pattern stored just below reading awareness. Imagine, for example, that you have been reading for several hours. Suddenly your attention is drawn from your reading to an awareness that something has changed. You immediately wonder what broke your concentration. However, before you can respond to your query, leaves rustle loudly outside your window. The "fight-or-flight" response of adrenaline takes charge, and you must ascertain whether you are in danger. Hearing the breezes and thunder of an approaching storm, you rise to peer out the window to check on the weather. Depending upon actual conditions, you choose to either return to your reading or seek shelter.

In this hypothetical case, consciousness, sensing a dramatic and potentially threatening situation, not only awakened you, but also brought you to an excited, heightened state of awareness. By bringing threatening stimuli to your attention, the subconscious mechanisms of the hindbrain served you well. Your consciousness is constantly monitoring your surroundings to ensure your safety. Pay attention to those vague stirrings that arise within you.

In the following exercise, notice how the applied focus to the breath vitalizes the body and enhances consciousness. When the kundalini breathing technique is done correctly, your consciousness has selected the body to be the primary focus while little attention is paid to the surroundings. Yet, there remains an underlying awareness that monitors your environment and surfaces when necessary.

KUNDALINI BREATHING TECHNIQUE

This exercise is to demonstrate a different use of breathing to produce energy in the physical body.

1. Find a comfortable sitting position on the floor with enough space to allow you freedom of movement. Sitting cross-legged balances the body as you do more vigorous movements. Use a pillow for comfort and support, as this will keep your feet from falling asleep.

2. Take a few deep, full breaths to change the focus from the outside world to the physical body containing your own inner awareness.

3. You may keep your eyes open or closed as you begin this breathing technique.

4. The arm movements are simple, but very powerful in changing the depth of breath. Practice them slowly at first until you develop the rhythm of the movements. Then you may increase the speed of the exercise.

5. With your next breath, inhale very deeply while bringing your arms straight up. Reach skyward, straighten the elbows, and extend the fingers as much as possible. Your arms are raised over your head while your shoulders remain down. This position allows the chest to lift and the lungs to expand.

6. When you can take in no more air, bring your arms down quickly while powerfully exhaling through your mouth. Close your fists as your arms move rapidly to their bent downward position. Keep the elbows close to your body, creating a powerful (rather than graceful) movement.

7. Practice the movements slowly until your body develops a rhythm. Gradually increase your speed to a rapid breath, trying to expend the same amount of energy in both inhalation and exhalation.

8. This type of breathing quickly creates heat in the body. Be moderate as you first begin this vigorous and stimulating practice. Limit practice to a five-minute sitting.

9. When you complete this exercise, notice how you feel. Is your body rejuvenated or fatigued? Does your head feel larger? Were you aware of the environment around you, or did the practice eliminate distractions? Are your senses more vivid afterward?

You may wish to integrate this breathing technique into your regular practice, as it provides a powerful focus. Some find it too overwhelming and only use it occasionally. Explore how it works best for you.

When exercising the physical body correctly, you will find that the limited focus also stimulates higher awareness. The natural order of the body is to use its resources through breath, exercise, sexuality, and other means to achieve heightened levels of consciousness. The initial emphasis is on the breath and posture to enhance the release of bodily energy to promote perception of more subtle energy vibrations.

Consciousness allows us to examine our response to stimuli. In the example of kundalini breathing, one level of consciousness actively performs the exercise while another guides us to notice the noise outside and explores the world for signs of danger. Another level is monitoring the well-being of the body.

Consciousness is frequently that subtle quiet internal voice that you hear alerting you that a loved one is about to telephone. If you are truly hungry, consciousness brings the hunger to your awareness. Hunger pangs can become too distracting and you may no longer be able to focus on breathing practices. This is your higher consciousness reminding you that it is time to take care of bodily needs by getting something to eat and drink. If, as in the case of the impending storm, you really are threatened, consciousness sends adrenaline into your system. Adrenaline prepares the body to escape or fight, whichever is appropriate to the situation. Notably, recent studies show that women respond more with a "tend-and-befriend" approach than the male-dominated "fight-or-flight" response. Consciousness reminds and directs your necessary actions. With experience in higher consciousness, you will find awareness of events before needing action. For example, you may sense and react to something being propelled toward you. These actions are coordinated long before you have time to think. The ability to do this does not come from intellectual knowing, but from a reliance on body consciousness. Try the following exercise.

GUIDING AND OVERSEEING ACTIONS EXERCISE

This exercise is best done in a casual environment—perhaps a cozy corner of your living room or a favorite conversation place outside. Seek the assistance of a good friend for this short exercise.

1. Bring a small object with you, such as a small foam ball, a ballpoint pen, or a small light object, and keep it at hand.

2. Engage your partner in conversation.

3. Without announcement and in a manner that surprises him or her, toss the object lightly in his or her direction. A typical response is to automatically either catch or deflect the object.

Often this is considered an automatic response. In this system, consider that higher consciousness is the faculty that oversees our actions and safety, and responds before thinking can occur.

SETTING PRIORITIES FOR ACTION

Consciousness ensures your survival by prioritizing your actions. As an infant, your consciousness had to develop survival mechanisms to attract attention so you could be nurtured. Whether it was food, touch, or attention you needed, you developed a system to attain the items and nurturing that assured your survival. Throughout your life, you have been gaining experience in obtaining what you need. First priority is given to essential items such as food, water, and shelter. Notice that when you are truly hungry—not just desiring to eat, but truly hungry—you can hardly think of doing anything else except obtaining food. When your body needs food, your blood sugar drops and your energy levels decrease. Survival always takes precedence, and the body shuts off less essential actions. As the provider for her cubs, even though a lioness provides milk and food, she must leave her cubs unprotected for a period of time to hunt food for herself. If she does not go out and kill, she will starve and her cubs will be left to their own fates. Despite the risk of leaving them unprotected, the lioness must leave to satiate her hunger. Her survival is top priority. Without her, her cubs have no chance of survival.

Fortunately, for most people in meditation circles, physical survival is already assured. Therefore, the elementary aspects of reasoning and logic are employed to determine that other activities such as sex, companionship, education, and entertainment are brought into awareness. For most readers, we have the luxury of being concerned with emotional well-being, happiness, and love. With these necessary elements of our lives fulfilled, then the exploration of intellectual interests, spiritual quests, and philosophic missions to find the meaning of life can begin. You are indeed fortunate to be a part of a society that allows you the freedom and resources to explore your interests.

DETECTING AND RESOLVING DISCREPANCIES

Human beings are creatures of habit. As part of our animal nature, the average person is constantly monitoring the environment. To understand this part of animal nature, consider a stallion grazing in a field. Though he munches happily, from time to time he will lift his head, look around, and verify that no coyotes have invaded his territory. With only the ability to run or kick in defense, his survival skills require him to constantly look for changes in his environment.

Similarly, human beings must look at change as potentially threatening. Consciousness constantly monitors and notes changes and discrepancies in the environment. Running in the background of our awareness is a feedback loop between outside stimuli and body responses in order to maintain a state of equilibrium. If you are familiar with chemistry, you may remember that an atom's electrons can be stimulated to change to different energy rings. To accomplish this, an atom must have some type of feedback system to determine its current state and its harmonious place in the environment. Is this quality consciousness? That is a question for your consideration.

The more evolved human being has varying options to resolve conflicts since it has at its disposal higher qualities such as intellect, intuition, and memory. A highly conscious being resolves change by comparing new events with known patterns. If the new event cannot fit into a known system, there is a tension created, which forces a change to expand the known world. For example, the boss may tell you that you need to become more of a team player, yet you know that you have contributed to the best of your ability to the team's success. Now you must find a new way to either highlight your contributions or to expand your ability to contribute by changing activities in order to meet your boss's expectations of a team player. The boss provides the tension since he or she evaluates your job performance, pays your salary, and maintains your employment. Tension and discrepancy are the major components to facilitate breakthroughs into new awareness of higher consciousness.

THE REALITY OF CONSCIOUSNESS

Consciousness is not an abstract concept, and can be felt by sensitized individuals. In the movie *The Highlander,* McCloud is in the audience of a wrestling match at Madison Square Garden. Surrounded by thousands of waving and cheering people, he sits unmoved. He is waiting. Pensive with heightened senses, he is expecting something else to happen. Ignoring the crowd and the ongoing match, he walks to the parking garage. There he senses a presence. Some aspect of higher consciousness alerts him to the approaching battle. While this is just a movie, such detection and knowledge of events is available in higher realms of consciousness.

In my own experience, I doubted whether these contacts in higher realms were real. I sought confirmation and proof by conducting a simple test at my teacher's home. My teacher was kneading bread dough in his kitchen, and he was surrounded by several students engaging him in conversation. The approach to his front door offered me a view into his kitchen window without being observed. Being in a highly conscious state, I gazed at him for only a few seconds before he pirouetted to see whom he felt.

Being of scientific mind, this wasn't good enough for me. If an experiment is successful, it should be repeatable, so I later performed the same test with exactly the same results. Mind you, this is not just looking at someone. It is *consciously* looking at someone with every energy center open, spirit radiating out of every pore, and with love for every aspect of being.

Hopefully, this next section will not apply to any of you, but again, like the warning on the cigarette package, I am compelled to inform you about the transitory experiences caused by drugs, near-death experiences, and exploitive initiations. While drugs, near-death experiences, and initiations may introduce a temporary state of high consciousness for some, the fully enlightened state may only be achieved through the hard work of removing all conditioning. Without conditioning, you have freedom to experience the totality of reality without being clouded by the haze of drugged thinking, or emotional or physical depletion. You can be in complete control of your faculties. Drugs and adrenaline highs also present the problem of addiction since one can easily achieve a temporary, possibly transcendent state. Choose instead to do the necessary spiritual work to achieve a permanent enlightenment.

In its purest form, meditation clears the mind to experience freedom in every moment. Meditation brings the awareness of the body, sensory input, thought, and the projection of the objects of mind into daily life. In the clear mind, there is an immense bliss, and an awareness of love and the interconnectedness to all life. Joyful understanding and knowing permeate life.

FOUNDATIONS OF MINDFULNESS

By now, you have become aware that there is an entire spectrum of consciousness in which you may become proficient. The experience of higher awareness in its own right may be addictive. Certainly, small successes reward the spiritual work and inspire continuance on the path of enlightenment.

In his shamanic books, Carlos Castaneda referred to these levels of consciousness as "bands of awareness." Other teachers use different terms and systems. However, if you complete any system of knowledge to its ultimate conclusion into mysticism, it is easy to relate all systems of truth. In my academic and esoteric studies, however, I have found that the Buddhist teachings on meditation are the simplest and hold true through many other systems. The Foundations of Mindfulness provide excellent guidelines on how to remain conscious through the complete spectrum of awareness. Specifically, the Satipatthana Sutta gives specific instructions to develop sustained awareness in four major areas: the body, sensations, mind, and objects of the mind.

In the first tenet of the Buddhist text, there are five explicit instructions for developing the sustained awareness of the body. At first, you allow the focus to be on the in and out rhythm of the breath. Simultaneously, whether standing, sitting, moving, or lying down, you must be clearly aware of the position of the body, and its effects on the breath. (You might note that this is similar to the relaxation technique in chapter 1.) The proper posture leads to meditation. Conversely, true meditation leads to proper position. If the body is aligned, it is effortless to sit in meditation. The energies of higher awareness move along the spine, relaxing the muscles while stimulating the mind to awaken. There have been times in my meditations when one vertebra popped into position much like a chiropractic alignment. Later, as you become more experienced in meditation you may explore how different postures and positions evoke different levels of awareness.

Extend this idea of mindfulness beyond the physical body to include the bodily functions (moving, eating, drinking, excreting, awakening, and so on). Every act of the body can be brought into our awareness. Certain yogis and certain biofeedback techniques use the mindfulness principle to lower blood pressure, control pain, and override autonomic body processes. Be mindful of the health of the physical body. You, as a practitioner of meditation, must understand how the only vehicle you have for expression, your human body, functions together as an integrated whole. Examine the taste of a fresh strawberry. Observe its color, feel its texture, taste its flavor. Notice how your experience of eating a strawberry changes as you slow down and observe the process while being mindful.

EXPANDED BREATHING MEDITATION

1. This exercise is best done in your regular meditation space. Find the posture that best allows you to breathe deeply and fully.

2. In many martial arts and religious traditions, breath is equated with life. Breath is an act that is absolutely necessary to life. Feel the air as you inhale it. Is it warm or cool? Sweet or unpleasant? Notice how you take air in, transform it within the body, and return it as a used, depleted element back to the environment. Breathe deeply.

3. Now, for a moment, imagine that you are the air being brought into the body, used to its fullest capacity, and then returned to the system from which it came. Breathe deeply and be the air that is life and spirit.

4. Breathe in this pattern until you feel the rhythm of being inside and outside of your body. For indeed, there is a parallel here. Being spirit, you enter the body, where you use the resources to the best

of your abilities. Then, when your work is done, you return to the system from which you came. Like the cycle of breath, you find the experience of the physical form to be a transitory experience. Breathe deeply and try to maintain that awareness as you open your eyes.

In mindfulness training, the body focus is important both in the nature of experiencing life and in addressing one of the greatest fears of humanity—death. Contemplating the death of the physical body while you continue to exist allows the perspective of the short time we have in form.

The second Buddhist principle in mindfulness addresses sensory experiences of physical reality. By concentrating on sense perception, you can notice how enhanced the senses become, and realize how much you normally filter out of your everyday awareness. Note your reaction to each of your senses. The subtlety of background sounds, the tastes and smells that linger with you, the texture of the carpet or floor, or the movement of air across your skin are all part of your awareness. Simple contemplation of the totality of your experience can reduce all events as being agreeable, disagreeable, or indifferent. Observe without judgment; just simply evaluate your reaction to the experience.

The sustained awareness of mind, perhaps the most difficult for the Western mind, is addressed in the third tenet of the Satipatthana Sutta. Here you begin to observe your moods or states of mind. The skill at which you are able to change from a bad mood into a pleasant one is the beginning exercise of being aware of the mind. Since the mind is easily distracted by the senses, the sustained awareness of mind is frequently practiced at silent retreats. However, once you attain this awareness, it should be integrated within all mundane tasks as well. Other practices often include the observation of repetitious events or tasks. For some, chanting engages body and mind while the awareness of both is enabled. For others, the concentration upon an object focuses the mind on a task, but allows awareness to continue on higher levels.

When I first experience this level, a song arises internally. In my mind, I sing silently and effortlessly without thinking in that mental realm. These beautiful songs are always on key, there is no searching for lyrics, and they fill my entire experience. However, if I do not focus on the song or the singing, the subtleties of awareness open and eventually the song disappears. Since I never heard anyone else report this phenomena, I considered these moments to be private failures in meditation. As I became more skilled in overcoming the distractions of the remembered songs of my early childhood, my teacher interjected a stimulating comment. In class discussion, he commented on the Christian hymns that frequently had arisen in my consciousness. Since I had never revealed that these songs were Christian hymns, I began to realize that higher consciousness knew no boundaries. My private meditation space was not just mine; it was shared by anyone conscious in those realms.

In the final instruction in mindfulness, you begin a sustained awareness of the mental experiences and all the lower levels are integrated within the meditator. The mind observes all things coming into existence, being, and then disappearing. All desires, thoughts, and concepts come into being, exist, and if the meditator is skilled, dissipate. The observed issues may be resolved within this realm so that they do not arise again in the future. Extraordinary sensory capacity is obtained: hearing is more sensitive, and the subtleties of scent and taste are accentuated. There is the knowledge of mindfulness, energy, tranquility, and equanimity. In the ultimate state of sustained awareness, the end of duality is known; the Creator and creation are one.

The instructions in the tenets of the Satipatthana Sutta are simple, but not necessarily easy. I recommend that you begin with the first step and continue with it until you can readily achieve it. Then proceed to the next stage. The process is slow, but steady. Mindfulness training leads you progressively through the stages of:

- Awareness of the body

- Awareness of the bodily sensations

• Awareness of the mind

• Awareness of the objects of the mind

If your progress begins to wane and you backslide, return to the first level of awareness of the body and begin the progression again. Even great concert pianists must occasionally return to the basic exercise of practicing scales. By repeating and reinforcing the basic techniques in meditation, your progress will once again begin moving forward.

While mindfulness is essential to the spiritual process, enlightenment cannot be achieved until self-completion. In one way, the concept of self-completion is misleading. While the focus is on obtaining a complete healthy self, you frequently cannot achieve this without the help of many others. My own experiences involved massage therapists, a great chiropractor, a former monk, some caring professors, trusting students, and an irritating teacher or two. Seek and follow the advice of those who are experts in their field. Simultaneously, find a working meditation group to share your progress. Peer support makes the journey both more enjoyable and more rapid.

The spiritual path is not an easy one, and few succeed in completing it. For me, the price in the early days was to incorporate minor changes in my life, but gradually rose over time to entirely change my focus. At first, my spiritual studies highlighted that I was generally dissatisfied with my materialistic life. I sought rewards through different avenues—relationships, spiritual discussions, and self-examination. Over time, I was motivated to renew myself in a different career direction. Through counseling, I resolved and healed traumas of divorce, trust, and insecurity. During later physical challenges, I continued undaunted to seek some elusive answer. Over the next years, I learned to give up attachments and found that my life is full and rewarding in many new ways.

Knowing that the spiritual journey to enlightenment will challenge you in every way, become the healthiest person you can be. With a firm healthy base, you are better prepared to explore alternative perceptions and realities. Otherwise, you risk your physical health, emotional stability, and possibly your sanity. If your life is in order, then it is time to introduce one of the most effective transformative tools available to humanity—meditation.

CHECK-IN EXERCISE

1. What areas of your life could use improvement and/or attention? What are you willing to change in order to have better health? What areas are you *un*willing to change? Why?

2. What would your ideal relationship look like? What can you do to achieve it?

3. What do you read? How are you continuing to learn in life?

4. What challenges excite you?

5. If you were told you had six months to live, what would you do? Why don't you do it now?

Chapter Three

MEDITATION STYLES

Meditation, like most forms of teaching, has evolved and adapted throughout its history as it plays a formative role in spiritual development and transformation in the world's religions and cultures. While no one really knows how formalized meditation practices began, the casual practice could have been as simple as gazing at the stars at night, pondering dreams, and wondering in pure quiet introspection. These meditative moments probably inspired queries beyond personal needs of the moment. From there, perhaps the insights gleaned stimulated a more structured discipline of meditation.

While meditation in its highest form is a way of being, the practice leading to it varies widely. No one method of meditation is more valid than another, as many practices lead to the highest state. Meditation practice is like climbing a mountain with many paths leading to its summit. Some people expend all their energy superficially exploring all the possible methods. They frequently end up circling the mountain, but never dedicate enough energy to climb it. Conversely, some people begin a path only to find that it switches back, and they must begin again at the bottom. Others doggedly follow a single path and manage to traverse the steep rocky slopes directly. At the mountain base, the paths of religion, ritual, and organization are diverse. Consequently, the choice of path to pursue is frequently difficult to determine. At the peak, where true understanding is achieved, it is easy to see that most trails lead up the mountain. The experience of the paths may be different, but their goals of achieving the summit are the same.

When beginning meditation, find a discipline that not only appeals to you, but that also serves you best. If you are intellectually inclined, explore a path that utilizes your keen mental development. However, if you are a natural athlete, you may find one of the movement meditations such as tai chi or yoga more natural to you. Since the road to full enlightenment is difficult enough anyway, play to your natural strengths.

It is often helpful to visit the past practices to better understand the present ones. A short review of meditation within established religions may not only provide an interest in cultural ritual and tradition, but may also establish a working vocabulary of alternative meditation practices. As a fundamental policy, students should be taught the terms of other traditions to compare and understand their experiences with others. In that way, comparison and contrast form a database of experience that is useful in the wisdom school's progressive meditation.

EASTERN ROOTS OF MEDITATION

Hinduism

In Hinduism, the way to God is through knowledge and the path of self-transformation. The practices of Hinduism create a change of identification from the individual identity, known as *atman,* to the true self within—equating to what could be called "becoming your higher self." With enlightenment, there is the realization that atman is Brahman, the supreme god. The individual is aware of both aspects: being a part of the divine whole, and of the individual aspects that participate in the physical world. In meditations, I use a similar metaphor of an individual raindrop that falls to earth to gain experience. Landing in a pool of water, the raindrop sends rings of awareness out along the larger body of water, which interacts and eventually absorbs its energy. The individualized raindrop can no longer be separate and distinguished; it follows the flow of the larger body. Water, consisting of thousands of raindrops, follows a different order and destiny as it progresses to the sea, where it assumes its role in the greater whole. Even there, though, the sun and heat evaporate the water into miniscule droplets of water vapor. Then, once again, as conditions permit, the raindrop can be separate. The raindrop is aware of its individual identity as well as its place in the infinite whole.

The ideal of an enlightened individual who holds both earthly and divine energies is not the only gift from the Hindu religion. The poetic songs of the Hindu Vedas (*Veda* means "to know") provide metaphors and beautiful descriptions of the transformative process to achieve that ideal. You read these songs aloud as they were intended to be read to reveal the underlying rhythm and melodic sounds. The meaning arises not only from the words, but also from the structure. Sounds are combined in such a way as to use the rhythmic breath in creative patterns. As you are already aware, breath is an integral part of life, and these songs provide multiple levels of teachings. Singing the Vedas reveals the pervasive influence of *rita*—the underlying order that naturally leads to the establishment of the natural sciences.

The Upanishads, on the other hand, are Hindu teachings that focus on the mind. *Upanishad* means "seated at the feet of the teacher," which implies that higher understanding involves an experiential component or energetic transmission from a more highly evolved being. The writings outline higher states of consciousness while exploring the sense of individuality, the flow of thought, and the search for a continuity of consciousness.

One teaching from the Upanishads suggests meditation focuses the attention inward by the use of pure concentration. This discipline requires a single-minded focus. Each time the mind wanders, the practitioner brings it back to its object of focus. This technique disciplines the mind. With enough practice, the mind doesn't wander and the intense focus awakens it to a transcendent state.

Knowing the senses to be separate
From the Self, and sense experience
To be fleeting, the wise grieve no more.
Above the senses is the mind,
Above the mind is the intellect,
Above that is the ego, and above the ego
Is the unmanifested Cause.
And beyond is Brahman, Omnipresent,
Attributeless. Realizing him one is released
From the cycle of birth and death.[1]

The Hindu doctrine not only focuses on the mind, but also on the physical body. In the Taittiriya Upanishad, the body is revealed as being multilayered, like the layers of an onion. Each layer of awareness of the body envelops different realms of mind. The senses, emotions, intellect, and will are all revealed and mark progressive stages on the meditative path. Finally, however, all that remains is consciousness or a complex force field. Time disappears along with death, and the self lives within the "body of joy." After self-realization, the immortality is attained; atman becomes brahman.

Yoga

The fertile Indus valley yielded another important practice—meditation through the physical body—yoga. First described by Pantanjali in the third century BCE, the practice of yoga spread rapidly. Yoga, meaning "to harmonize or unite," incorporates the body with the highest level of consciousness to realize the true self of the heart. While the developments in various methods, styles, and applications of yoga can comprise an entire book, they all share the goal of realizing the divine within the physical.

In the yogic philosophy, where the mind is stilled and the body centered, consciousness reflects the absolute spirit, or *purusa*. Purusa

---

1. Eknath Easwaran, *The Upanishads* (Tomales, Calif.: Nilgiri Press, 1987), 95–96.

encompasses a timeless quality with a quiet inner peace. When this state is maintained, there is liberation from the temporal world, *mokṣa.* A mind liberated from the attachments of the mundane world is enlightened.

Yogic discipline starts with *asanas*—postures held while allowing the mind to abstract from the body. Some yoga forms use breath control, or *pranayama,* to reach various levels of consciousness. Pranayama today includes varied breathing exercises: slowing the breath by counting to a set number in both inhalation and exhalation, alternately holding one nostril closed during each breath, and concentrating on the point of the breath where inhalation reverses to exhalation. Experimentation with pranayama produces tangible, reproducible results. Gradually, yoga allows the mind to withdraw from the limitations of sensory input, and concentration deepens.

Another technique is to focus on a single object, such as a candle's flame or a guru. This single pointed focus develops extraordinary concentration abilities. Every time the mind drifts away from the object, the meditator brings it back to concentrate on a single image. After some time and practice, the state of *samadhi,* the complete cessation of all modifications of mind, may be achieved. The transcendent state of samadhi with the awareness of purusa is a state of ecstasy and enlightenment.

While there are many forms of yoga with varying purposes, there is one particular path, Kundalini yoga, which many teachings utilize. The Upanishads suggest the use of desire as the major source of energy in the self-transformation process. The most powerful and universally available of these desires is the human sexual drive. While the physical sexual act was considered sacred, the religious teachings do not forbid it. The Upanishads suggest living in the world with your passions under control, not controlling you. In Kundalini yoga, or *kriya* yoga, the inherent sexuality of the body awakens the consciousness to higher awareness. Energetic centers resembling wheels or spheres, known as *chakras,* circulate the higher energies into physical form. By awakening the serpent goddess Kundalini, who progresses upward through the body to unite with the god Siva, the yogi and the cosmos resolve into the state of oneness at the crown chakra. This highly catalytic form of yoga should only be practiced with the proper instructor and preparation.

Kundalini and the Chakra System

There are many systems of energy, but for convenience, only the yoga system of chakras will be introduced, as it has universal applications. Chakras, a Sanskrit word meaning "disks in movement" or "wheels," receive, assimilate, and transmit energies into the physical body. Although there are many chakras, only an overview of the seven major chakras, shown in figure 1, will be discussed in this book.

In the Kundalini yoga system, the divine energy referred to as "the goddess Kundalini" exists both in the cosmic and personal form. When the divine energy is to incarnate, the personal aspect of the divine oversees the development of the human fetus. After conception, the head and brain of an embryo are formed; next, the nervous system branches from the brain into the development of the spinal cord. Subsequently, additional chakras are formed as the body's trunk and extremities develop. Kundalini, initiating creation at the brain, progresses downward along the spinal column and completes the seventh stage of her work at the base of the spine, where she rests.

Spiritual evolution of the human begins when the sleeping serpent goddess Kundalini awakens and rises in the maturing body. Frequently this awakening is stimulated by the release of hormones at puberty. If unimpeded, Kundalini's upward journey energizes and enlightens each chakra in succession until she reaches the crown of the head. The qualities of each chakra are intensified by her touch.

For many people, the process of awakening is thwarted at puberty. Only when the individual is ready to continue the inherent spiritual evolution is the Kundalini process stimulated. To invoke the healing powers of the goddess, toning, visualization, and energetic stimulation of the chakra system are frequently used in ritual catharsis. Kundalini awakening profoundly affects consciousness at each chakra she

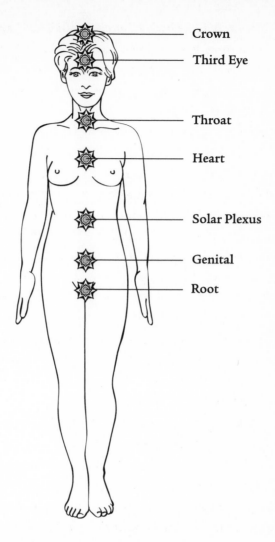

Figure 1: Representation of chakra location.

touches. Much as puberty is an unknown process to the innocent child, Kundalini awakening provides challenges and changes in the adult. Some people have described intense heat, strange visions, and amazing insights as Kundalini progresses through the chakras. In the final enlightenment, all chakras fuse into a continuous flow of divine energy through the human body.

The chakra system as it is described here is derived not only from its Hindu roots, but also includes numerological, alchemical, and biological aspects as a point of reference for your work. Each chakra, beginning with the resting place of Kundalini in the base of the spine, can become the focus of your meditation and reveal aspects of your own divinity. See table 1 for qualities associated with each chakra.

Chakra	Location	Associated Quality	Color	Sound
1	base of spine	survival issues, earth	red	oh
2	lower abdomen	sexuality, desire, water	orange	oo
3	solar plexus	will power, fire	yellow	ah
4	heart	love	green	ay
5	throat	communication	blue	ee
6	forehead, third eye	intuition, dreaming	indigo	om, mm
7	crown	thought, spirituality	violet	ngngng

Table 1: Chakras and their associated qualities.

The root chakra represents individualization from the divine and is assigned the numerical association of the number 1, which symbolizes the initial differentiation from the primal sea. In numerology, this chakra is the birth from the wholeness of the sea (the sea is sometimes considered to be the great Mother of all life) to the singularity of the individual. The associated elements of the root chakra are the fruits of the earth that enable the survival of the individual—food, shelter, and water. The active, or masculine, creation process of the base chakra promotes individuality that arises from the primordial whole.

The second chakra, located at the procreative organs—the ovaries or testicles—introduces the concept of duality. Numerically represented as 2, duality is obvious in the separation of the creative force into male and female physical bodies. The activation of the sexual center in an individual stimulates the emotional needs and desire to combine in order to restore unity. Through the second chakra's influence of the element of water, you may discover a flow of emotions, the need for nurturing, and the quest to unite with your opposite. Sexuality is a powerful force that desires to resolve separateness and propels the continuation of life. Wilhelm Reich's scientific and pioneering efforts into the use of sexual energy for healing were not well received in the early 1900s, but many modern alternative healing methods base their work on his utilization of procreative forces.

The desire for unification created in the second chakra fuels the upward journey of Kundalini to the fiery third chakra of transformation. Located at the solar plexus, the third chakra houses energy and power. While the elements of earth and water of the first and second chakra naturally gravitate downward, fire burns upward toward air. Here the trinity of the individual and the desire of the couple results in the reunification of two into a third. The procreative force develops only in the union of opposites. Similarly, in the golden light of the third chakra, the desires and emotions of the two lower chakras combine to stimulate the fiery drive for transformation.

The opening of the heart at the fourth center brings to mind the phrase, "Love is all you need." The heart center, sharing the numerical association of 4 with the earth plane of existence, focuses on relationships and the interconnection of all life. The ego is transcended and love radiates in all directions. The air element of the fourth chakra provides the missing ingredient for the burning fire of the third chakra. Consider love pouring down from the heart to assist the process of transformation in the third chakra. Love's unconditional acceptance allows the bonds of the ego to be transcended for the first time. Similarly, the heart chakra mediates between the realm of the personal chakras (1, 2, and 3) and the transpersonal chakras (5, 6, and 7). Love is experienced in all four directions in the four corners of the world.

With love comes the desire to share in its experiences. As Kundalini continues to rise, the throat chakra, the center of communication, awakens. In the fifth chakra, associated with the number of the goddess, the power of language, the arts, and vibration extend outward. Through the communication of the fifth chakra with the world, you may begin to participate in your personal evolution of consciousness.

As Kundalini pierces the sixth chakra at the center of the forehead, intuition, vision, and dreaming penetrate everyday awareness. The sixth chakra is commonly referred to as the "third eye" because it perceives light directly. Just as the eyes interpret the data of the physical world, the third eye processes the information of the spiritual realm. The third eye is highly developed in clairvoyants who inherently see reality in a far different way than most. Simultaneously, the awakening of the sixth chakra also stimulates the higher yogic forms of dreaming; sleep is permeated with spiritual awareness and communication between highly conscious human beings may occur.

Finally, Kundalini reaches her destination to join her consort, Shiva, at the crown chakra, where consciousness and enlightenment reside. The element of thought completes the knowledge of the physical world, and expands awareness into the whole cosmos. All truth is known. The crown chakra is a dimensionless point of awareness. The goddess has not only descended into the world of matter, but she has also returned to the world of spirit, carrying the wisdom of her experiences in form.

Kundalini then reconnects to the universal qualities of the eighth chakra outside of the physical body. In dimensions beyond those of space and time, she achieves the mystical connection of the nonphysical ninth chakra. Kundalini, as she embraces the cosmic within the physical, becomes the number ten, which combines the state of emptiness and unity. The number ten begins a new cycle through the archetypal progression. Kundalini is the catalyst to combine the infinite with the realized individual.

Enlightenment occurs when the journey through the chakras is completed, and you have fully integrated wisdom, truth, and clarity within your being. Finally, you encounter total reality, absolute truth, and complete knowledge of the self.

Bhagavad Gita

Another important contribution from India is the Bhagavad Gita, "song of the blessed one." Here, Prince Arjuna discusses philosophy with the avatar Krishna on the eve of the battle of Armageddon. Topics covered are karma, reincarnation, yoga, freedom, and life; all are still pertinent today.

India has mythological themes that encompass the entire spectrum of human interaction. Deep within her traditions are the ebb and flow of the rhythm of the cosmos, the transformation of the human, and living in harmony. Make time to read some of these exquisite texts aloud.

> It is not those who lack energy or refrain from action, but those who work without expectation of reward who attain the goal of meditation. Theirs is true renunciation. Therefore, Arjuna, you should understand that renunciation and the performance of selfless service are the same. Those who cannot renounce attachment to the results of their work are far from the path.[2]

Buddhism

Buddhism, currently the religion most closely associated with meditation, incorporates the practice of meditation to penetrate the veil of illusion. The meditative discipline is instrumental in unraveling the conditioning of *samsara,* or this mundane world. Only by breaking through the conditioning may true reality be perceived. If a meditator finds a way of being that perceives reality directly, there is escape from *reincarnation,* the karmic cycle of birth, death, and rebirth. This liberated state, known as *nirvana,* is the goal of Buddhist meditation.

Nirvana etymologically means "to extinguish," a confusing term to the English language. In the metaphor of fire, you can imagine a state

---

2. *The Bhagavad Gita,* trans. Eknath Easwaran (Tomales, Calif.: Nilgiri Press, 1987), 104.

where, deprived of fuel, the fire goes out. In nirvana, all desires have been consumed and everything restricting boundless life has been annihilated. With this understanding, nirvana is the highest destiny of humanity. The Buddha gave only one affirmative response to the characterization of nirvana: "Bliss, yes bliss, my friends, is nirvana."[3]

In the Dhammapada, a popular Buddhist text, the opening words are: "All we are is the result of what we have thought." It continues with "all things can be mastered by mindfulness."[4] Mindfulness, the foundation of Buddhist meditation, includes the *samatha*, or mindfulness practice. Devoted samatha leads into the advanced practice of *dhyana*, or meditative absorption. The dhyanas are a gradual progression of identified stages of meditation without the verbal, discursive, and affective contents of the mind. The dhyanas are attained only when you transcend the mental functions. Beyond the four dhyanas is the formless realm, a state beyond all sense data. This final realm is infinite consciousness and infinite space.

Like many great teachers, the Buddha, the awakened one, never committed his teachings to written forms. His teachings given over a forty-five year time span were recorded approximately 150 years after his death. The interpretations and interpolations led to two distinct forms of Buddhism: Theravada and Mahayana. In Theravada Buddhism, progress is determined by the resolute application to the path. Mahayana Buddhism is a less formal eclectic form of Buddhism that usually includes the Buddhist schools in Tibet, China, and Japan. A major doctrinal difference is the concept of salvation. In Mahayana Buddhism, a bodhisattva, a person who renounces the final entry into nirvana to facilitate enlightenment for all sentient beings, embodies that principle.

Salvation is the primary goal for the Pure Land School of Buddhism as well. The Pure Land is a realm where the practitioner hopes

---

3. Houston Smith, *The World's Religions* (San Francisco: HarperSanFrancisco, 1992), 114.

4. *Anguttara Nikaya,* 8:83.

to be reborn after death. There is no retrogression in a Pure Land; all the spiritual accomplishment of a lifetime is retained, which alleviates the problem of having to start from scratch in the next life. Acceptance into the Pure Land, where everything is purified of samsara or space-time defilements, provides assistance from the infinite light of Amitabha Buddha. Sincere utterance of Amitabha's name three times is adequate admission to the lower hierarchy of the Pure Land: Om namo Amitabha. Om namo Amitabha. Om namo Amitabha. The compassion of Amitabha has yielded the slogan of Pure Land Buddhism as the "easy path to enlightenment."

Tibetan Buddhism, greatly influenced by the native shamanic Bön religion, uses elaborate visualizations of deities, stylized rituals, and devotional meditation. This form of worship consists of reciting prayers and sacred texts, and chanting hymns to the accompaniment of horns, trumpets, and drums. Lamas perform rites with the use of *malas* (similar to rosaries), prayer wheels, and prayer flags. Rituals also utilize holy relics, charms, and talismans. Some sacred artwork depicts specific postures known as mudras, which, when contemplated or held, transmit or receive inspired or energetic transmissions. With the imposed exile from Tibet, the monks and their spiritual leader, the Dalai Lama, have brought their once-secret traditions of their religion to the world.

Zen Buddhism is the result of the progression of Buddhism out of India into China and Tibet, and then into Japan. Zen, a transliteration of the Sanskrit term *dhyana* into *Ch'an* in China that in turn was translated into *Zen* in Japan, literally means "seated meditation." Zen meditation emphasizes sitting in formless awareness. In the halls of meditation, monks devote hours to sitting in the lotus posture silently. The eyes are kept half shut and softly gazing on a spot on their mats extending before them. The instruction is to observe thoughts, feelings, and visions that may come into consciousness, and then allow them to pass away. Zen meditation is a state of no-mind, where there is no grasping of thoughts or feelings.

Zen renounces both theorizing and meditation systems to answer all philosophic or religious questions. The answer is always that the action is just as it is, and not what it represents. Unlike other forms of Buddhism, Zen holds that such freedom of mind cannot be attained by gradual practice, but must come through direct and immediate insight, called *satori*. Satori is the Zen version of the mystical state. All the seated meditations lead to a widening of the doors of perceptions that enable awareness to flow into the mundane world. When the meditator is able to detach from both external and internal stimuli, there is a state of stillness, emptiness, and awareness.

The Zen practice does employ an extremely valuable tool on the way to the state of emptiness, the *koan,* which is an extremely absurd problem a Zen aspirant is given to contemplate. For example, "What is the sound of one hand clapping?" The full concentration of the mind is directed on the koan. Often logic must be abandoned in order for the mind's innermost process to evolve an acceptable answer. In resolving this paradoxical puzzle, the Zen practitioner provokes, excites, and finally exasperates the mind's mental process. At that moment of mental exhaustion or transcendence, a flash of insight bridges the understanding.

Progress toward a clear mind is also assisted by *sanzen,* a consultation between student and teacher. These brief meetings allow the student to state the current progress toward resolving the koan and to receive direction from the master. If the answer is correct, the master performs the redundant act of validating it. The truth of a correct answer provides its own validation. The more beneficial role of the master is to reject inadequate answers. The student is examined closely for false conceptions, immaturity, and prejudices. The master may then direct the student in ways to energize and purify in an expedient manner.

Taoism

Taoism embodies the ultimate principle of mysticism—a state of being beyond phenomenal manifestations and yet within which all phenomenal manifestations are brought forth and undergo change.

Taoism cultivates your wholeness of being with the wholeness of the universe.

Much of Taoism is based on the *Tao-Te Ching* and the writings of Lao-Tzo and Chuang-Tzo. The Tao means "the road" or "the Way." In Taoist doctrine, heaven and earth follow immutable laws where there is a constant contrast between mundane reality and the Taoist sage's viewpoint. In both Lao-Tzo and Chuang-Tzo's philosophy, a person transcends an egocentric cosmic viewpoint to a holistic one. In doing so, the Tao seeks only to conform to the underlying pattern of the universe. The mystical verse of the opening chapter of the *Tao-Te Ching* best expresses its philosophy:

> The Tao that can be told is not the Eternal Tao;
> The name that can be named is not the eternal name.
> The Nameless is the origin of Heaven and Earth;
> The Named is the mother of all things.[5]

The Taoists envision a multilayered body and incorporated ideas of internal alchemy in their transformation process. By stripping away the outer realms, it is possible to reach the final immortal body. Issues or resistance that block the bodily flow of *chi*, essential life energy, must be worked through so that the underlying energy channels connect. Some traditional Chinese medicines work with the body's meridians or energy channels.

> One is all.
> All is one.
> When you take no sides for the one or all,
> There is nothing that cannot be dissolved in the Subtle Origin.
> Follow the absolute Way.
> The universal absolute mind never separates from anyone,
> But the people go astray.

---

5. Hua-Ching Ni, *The Taoist Inner View of the Universe and the Immortal Realm* (Seven Star Communications Group, 1996), 156.

> When one attains absolute-mindedness,
>
> Words and concepts cease to exist.
>
> In the great integrity,
>
> There is no past, future, or present.[6]

The beautiful poetry and clarity of Taoist writings and philosophy are highly recommended reading.

MEDITATION IN WESTERN RELIGION

Judaism

The doctrines of Judaism are based on both written and oral teachings. The Talmud, a record of two thousand years of oral teaching, is an aggregation of law, parable, and philosophy. In the Talmud, God's will continues to unfold. These oral teachings require concentrated listening; there must be a concerted effort to remain totally in the moment. You might apply those skills when listening to lectures or informative programs. With modern recording devices, most people forget the applied listening skills and concentration that develop a disciplined mind.

The written Judaic tradition required different concentrative techniques, and two unique forms of meditation are utilized: single-minded concentration and discursive meditation. In reading the Torah, the sacred mystical text comprised of the five books of Moses, there must be a total focus on the literal words of this practical book of instruction. For example:

> Turn it over and over, for it contains everything. Keep your eyes riveted to it. Spend yourself in study. Never budge from it, for there is no better life than that.

Conversely, since it is a mystical text as well, there is an esoteric meaning available to a reader at a higher awareness. When reading the

---

6. Hua-Ching Ni, *The Taoist Inner View of the Universe and the Immortal Realm* (Seven Star Communications Group, 1996), 156.

Torah, there can be a free-flowing association that links one idea to another. Examine the literal translation of those words and then look for more. Is something that contains everything a thing that can be turned over? Are there sides to wholeness? Spend life in study, never budging from it. Does this mean that the study is worth more than experience? Is gaining knowledge then the only answer for a good life? Where is the wisdom behind the words and how do you find it?

Using these questions to explore ideas, some faculty higher than normal intellect links the relationship between your ideas. This, in turn, forms a higher understanding of a fundamental truth. This discursive method builds on such realizations, then the relationships between the realizations can be linked to formulate higher wisdom, creating a spiral of evolving wisdom. The Jewish mystic can use this circle of self-understanding in personal transformation. In achieving such clarity through extensive discursive meditation, Jewish mystics may develop the capacity to realize the original goal of Judaism—to see and hear God directly.

As Judaism evolved over time, the ability to see and hear God directly was not limited to the Jewish mystic. This mystical attainment was virtually guaranteed by the roots of the Hasidic cult of Judaism, which arose in the first century CE and promoted devotion over intellectual study. The Hasidics promised that on the day of Yahweh (at the end of this world) all would achieve a direct contemplation of God.

All religions require continual adaptations to accommodate changing social, political, and cultural conditions if they are to survive. Of course, the very adaptations that ensure their survival may also be their demise. The mystery schools were lost when Christianity adopted many of their festivals, holidays, and traditions. So, alternately, there is also consideration to maintain the traditional ways. Within Judaism arose new schools of thought. A new Judaic meditation system arose in the Qabalistic School of the thirteenth century CE. In the Qabala (the name means "received tradition") each letter of the alphabet is regarded as a constituent of the holy name of God. The combination of letters, without conscious intent to form words, allows the formation of a mystical logic. The combination of shapes and sounds without having the vowels specified allow multilevel meaning. The ultimate achievement for the Qabalistic adept is the pure contemplation of the divine name. The study of the Qabala today provides esoteric maps, such as the Tree of Life, to higher wisdom. There are many rituals and teachings that the Judaic religion provide as a foundation for Western prayer, meditation, and contemplation.

Christianity

From its Judaic roots, Christianity adopted meditation as well as the theme of the mystical knowledge of God. Plotinus, an Egyptian philosopher (200 CE), outlined a progression of stages one must accomplish in order to know God. These stages included purifying methods, the removal of negativity by the practice of virtue, the use of meditation to achieve knowledge beyond sensory perception, and an ultimate absorption into the one God. The use of meditation was further expanded when in third-century Alexandria, a sect of Christian Gnostics used meditation to include the exploration of other intelligible realities. Their meditation techniques were combined with *gnosis,* a gift from Christ that led to a mystical awareness.

The Jesuits further refined the progressive form of meditation when Ignatious Loyola (sixteenth century) presented his outline of the meditation stages. Meanwhile, his contemporary, Teresa of Avila, a member of the Carmelite order, wrote her outline of progressive ecstatic meditative stages in the imagery of the bridal couple. She describes the initial meeting, the betrothal, and the consummation of the married couple.

Similarly, St. John of the Cross refined the bridal symbolism into stages of clearing (retained), betrothal (illumination), and spiritual marriage (union). Through his other work, the phrase "Dark Night of the Soul" has made it into Western culture. The Dark Night of the Soul occurs when you reach something so divine and wonderful and are unable to maintain that level of consciousness. You feel the despair of wondering whether you will ever find that state of grace again.

Many people classify it as depression; the symptoms are very similar. The world appears very dark with no meaning or purpose. You have no interest in anything except, if you can remember it, finding this higher awareness. This stage, too, will pass.

Early Christianity embraced an austere lifestyle, prayer offerings, and quiet contemplation on the scriptures. Even today, meditation or moments of silence are frequently offered within church services. You will find meditation, healing circles, and even yoga offered within the Christian church. A religion must adapt to its culture's changing trends in order to remain viable.

Islam

Muslims, members of the Islamic faith, embrace their religion into their daily lives. Their spiritual doctrines often directly influence the political, cultural, and community life. Prayers as remembrances of God are done openly in the community. It is not uncommon to hear the call to prayer from the mosque in Muslim communities or to have shopkeepers pull out their prayer rug during store hours. While the Western media frequently focuses on the radical factions of Islam, you are encouraged to search for other balancing views of Islamic practice. Knowledge is the antidote to fear.

Within orthodox Islam, Sufism, a form of mysticism, arose to challenge traditional teachings. The Sufi approach to God was one of ecstatic love and the desire for union. Using meditation, dance, song, and *dhikr,* the Sufis find transcendence from the mundane world. In a dhikr, poetry, chants, and even music are shared, and participants also practice breath control, repetition of sounds, and the visualization of sacred words as a contemplative practice. Such devotional practices lead one to *fana,* the annihilation of the lower self. You might compare this process to becoming your higher self. At that stage of release, the purification of the mystic prepares the way for the union with the Beloved, or the divine. At that moment, God may bestow grace upon the mystic and unification occurs.

In a specialized form of Islam, the whirling dervishes of the Mevlevi order employ sacred dance as a meditation practice. Created from the teachings of Rumi in the thirteenth century, the dance is controlled by the *shayk,* or Sufi leader. With a nod, a slight movement of his foot, or a simple gesture, the shayk indicates the position, speed, and length of the movements. Keeping the left foot as a fixed pivot, the dervish spins to hypnotic music and chanted poetry. The Sufi is transported to a heightened state of consciousness, as are those who feel the patterns of the whirling energies. The devotional aspects of Sufism produce a centered and concentrated awareness.

HISTORICAL SUMMARY

Presenting historical material is vital to establishing a common vocabulary for meditation as well as stimulating interest in exploring the world's traditions. As meditation practitioners mature into teachers, they should have an understanding of the past before moving forward—especially if these conscious people are to become functional mystics to take on roles of conscious cocreators of the future.

These brief synopses of the religious forms of meditation are far from comprehensive, but are intended to provide you with a working meditation vocabulary from various traditions. Even with that disclaimer, it should also be noted that no description of these meditative states could compare with the experience of them. Meditation with a qualified teacher is the single most valuable tool in the process of self-transformation. The truth is inherent within many religious traditions. By focusing on the truth, all doctrines become pathways to the divine.

Chapter Four

THE MEDITATION MAP
& FORMING GROUPS

FORM AND FORMLESS MEDITATION

Now that you have a background of the various types of meditation, it may be helpful to begin relating these styles. For simplicity, you can categorize meditation into two major categories: formless and progressive. These styles are radically different; formless allows an unstructured experience, while the progressive technique establishes distinctly identifiable stages of awareness. However, both formless and progressive meditations share the ultimate goal of creating an enlightened being. It is only the style that differs. When working with a group seeking personal and collective transformation, I employ a combination of both styles when and where it is appropriate.

On the occasions when I inform acquaintances that I teach meditation, most respond with questions on either transcendental meditation or Zen Buddhism, since both forms have filtered into the awareness of mainstream society. Formless meditation is epitomized in Zazen, a form of sitting meditation done as naturally as possible. The only instruction necessary for sitting meditation is to simply observe, without mental comment, whatever may be happening. While the instruction is simple, the practice isn't easy. Consequently, I often teach this formless type of meditation in the early morning when it is more easily achieved. Students, before becoming involved in routine activities, usually haven't engaged the intellect fully, and the needs of the body haven't yet begun to interfere.

In some formal Zen practices, a master, fully conscious of everyone's process, walks among practitioners with a stick. When observing someone caught in thought, ego, or daydreams, the master raps the person across the shoulders to remind him or her to return to the clear, calm state of observation. The stick may also become a teaching instrument in personal sittings as well. This may be a very useful practice for the beginner and/or the advanced student; however, ultimately you must take the responsibility to monitor your own state of awareness and learn to maintain the high clarity of meditation without assistance.

The Zen meditator's goal is the highest state of consciousness, the one that was attained by the Buddha. The Buddha mind is free of the individuality of self, and perceives the true nature of reality. Consequently, Zen is frequently called the "no-mind" state of consciousness, since thoughts arise and depart without a trace. This perfected Zen state is the end product of many repetitious hours and for most people may simply be a transitory experience. Yet, once achieved, the state of "no-mind" is much easier to attain again. Frequent, even brief, achievement in regular practice eventually leads to a continuous meditative state.

Progressive meditation utilizes a much different approach; you take apart what you intend to consciously reunite. The wholeness of awareness is separated into a journey of progressive meditation that leads you from one stage of development to the next. When enlightenment is achieved, it is easy to see that all these processes are simply divisions of the whole. Progressive meditation can be compared to a worm's journey through an orange. To reach all sections of the whole, the worm must travel through each segment, traverse the membrane that separates them, and continue through all the sections until it returns to the origin. The worm will have an in-depth experience of the orange, not just an outside examination of the whole.

Though formless and progressive meditations share the goal of the awakened mind, their methods are vastly different. Progressive steps enrich the process of meditation and prove very effective with achievement-oriented Western students. Since some established groups simply sit together in meditation with a teacher and depart without saying a word, newcomers often feel frustrated. Neither the format nor the teaching makes it easy to determine if the students are meditating correctly. Rarely, though, students may sit with a group or teacher to meditate and leave with such a heightened awareness that there is no doubt that they were in the midst of a shared higher consciousness. While it is possible to learn from a master through energetic transmission alone, progressive meditation provides tangible goals and achievements along the path as feedback.

The goal of progressive meditation, like that of the Zen Buddhist, is a perfected state of consciousness. The approach to progressive meditation is one of conscious volition versus the Zen-type observation. Many students find the formless practices too easy to get lost in; consequently, some mainstream approaches provide guided visualizations and imagery. Some of these techniques are useful for relaxation and stress reduction, but have little value in understanding the process of meditation and awareness. The preparatory training in progressive meditation molds awareness, body, mind, and emotions for the complete understanding of the ultimate realm of consciousness. This meditation discipline also teaches the use, function, and achievement of every identified realm of consciousness. The progressive form builds upon the foundation of the layer below it. Consequently, the attainment of a level embraces all functions of the realms beneath it. The progressive meditation process fully engages all that makes you human, and allows you to know the self in all its aspects. The mechanisms also allow progressive meditation's transformative process to be taught to others, which makes it an invaluable tool in the evolution of consciousness.

Progressive meditation does not require the abandonment of human faculties (such as the senses) that process reality. Instead, it is the discovery of new, less specialized, and more embracing ways to contact reality. When you become a dynamic meditator, you use specialized human abilities. Ultimately, even these talents must be abandoned in order to practice without limitation.

The discipline of progressive meditation mechanics establishes a map of the territory of consciousness. Maps enable understanding levels of consciousness that exist, but may be as yet unrecognized. Each stage of meditation employs universal markers that identify its quality. With a proven map and recognizable markers, you can compare your meditation with that of a teacher who has already surveyed the territory.

For example, imagine being led into a strange room late at night. Suddenly the lights go out. In the pitch-black darkness, you cannot see the room's contents or how to exit. You might have a brief recollection of what you initially saw, but without light, you are unsure that there is anything there. When you move, you bump into unexpected objects. After a while, unless you stumble onto the exit, your fear of the unknown may prevent you from moving at all. Then your teacher, as a guide who knows the layout of the darkened room, says, "Take my hand and walk with me." Together, walking within the protection of someone else's radiance, you begin a journey to find your own light to illuminate your way. Then as you negotiate your way to the light switch, you bump into a seemingly impenetrable wall. Your teacher, knowing and seeing the way, shows you the secret passage through. As you reach the light switch, the teacher assists you in turning the light on. All is revealed and you are able to see what you have just walked through. You are enlightened.

In this metaphor, the entrance into the room signifies your initiation into a new realm of consciousness. This foreign territory is difficult to negotiate the first time. The use of a teacher's map or direct guidance, however, facilitates an exploration of a space without running into too many obstacles. When you do encounter a problem, the teacher's experience with those barriers allows you to overcome them with relative ease. Finally, the teacher illuminates the entire room so that you become more familiar with the entire realm. Later, when you negotiate that consciousness level on your own, you remember the markers pointed out and the way through that realm of consciousness. A teacher's meditation map brings the unrecognized consciousness out of the darkness and into the light.

Throughout esoteric history, there have been different schemes for the maps of consciousness. One map type resembles an onion that starts at the core and progresses outward like sheaves of different refinements of energy: the further away from the body, the more refined, since those levels are less materialistic. As you move farther in toward the core, the levels become denser. Another map resembles a step pyramid with smaller, higher layers building upon each other with some interpenetration. The map used in the wisdom school teachings and my research resembles the step pyramid model. Beginning with a broad base, the energy is collected and focused so that the next level is built on top of the base. Imagine that the weight of the top sinks that layer into the previous foundation. Each subsequent layer assimilates energy and consciousness to build a platform for subtler levels of awareness. Finally, the peak realm is achieved by building on all the layers below it.

Still other consciousness schemes follow a linear path. The Major Arcana series of the traditional tarot deck, an example of a straightforward journey, originates with a fool embarking on a journey of self-discovery. The major archetypes, such as the Emperor, the Tower, Death, the Lovers, and so on, delineate stages on the spiritual path that create opportunities for change and growth. Step-by-step, one foot after the other, the Fool continues the journey until she emerges as the Universe, the final card of the Major Arcana. While the progression is linear, the completion of the tarot path progression reveals its own circularity. This Fool card of the Major Arcana is frequently marked as the card of origin and completion by being numbered 0–22.

Most meditation and transformation systems begin very differently, but share a common goal to reach the pinnacle of consciousness, the mystical state. Like hikers trying to attain the summit of a mountain, you follow the path staked out by others who have gone before you. The well-trodden path gradually ascends into higher realms of consciousness. There are forks in the path and alternative avenues to explore. Eventually, most of these paths converge at the summit where you can see the parallel paths leading to the top, and realize that the mystical state knows no boundaries.

The most difficult aspect when just beginning meditation is to learn how to initiate the process. Personally, I sat with many teachers without realizing the true awareness that meditation reveals. However, once I sat with my meditation master, I immediately felt the difference. A clarity and depth emerged that I had never felt before. There is no easy way to explain this to another unless he or she has had a similar experience. Many people practice for years without knowing what meditation really is. Once properly introduced or initiated, however, there is an enriched reality of meditation. Meditation, beyond a beginner's introduction to relaxation and visualization, progresses more quickly with a qualified teacher. A teacher may direct the transformative energies to benevolently open the doors of perception. Once you experience its fullness, all techniques, instructions, art, and writings take on enriched meaning.

FINDING A MAP OF THE TERRITORY

When my teacher introduced me to the idea of differentiating levels in meditation, I thought he was crazy. My natural proclivity is the formless style of meditation, but he persisted in drilling students for hours in what I considered a senseless game. Being bored during these interminable sessions, I decided I had nothing better to do and began to learn his techniques. Subsequently, I was richly rewarded. I was able to observe and quantify the techniques that he used in a purely energetic fashion. By recreating these observed energetic patterns, I created my own database of techniques with documented results.

In my recreation of the meditation stages with my own groups, the progressive levels are identified as everyday awareness, the astral, the archetypal, the essences, the void, the triad, and the absolute. Part of this work developed a history of the entire spectrum of human ability to recognize consciousness. Note that progress in meditation is circular and you may enter or leave the circle at any point or traverse in either direction. If you are familiar with Buddhist teachings, you might find a comparison of this cycle to the Buddhist twelve stage circle of causation interesting. It shares circularity as well as progression.

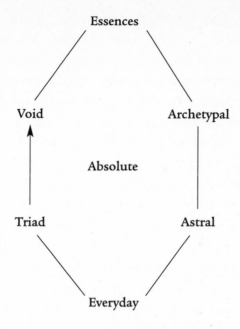

Figure 2: The Great Circle of Meditation.

The great circle of meditation (see figure 2) is a teaching mechanism that is best explored within working meditation groups. These groups are not just an assembly of attendees, but are carefully constructed organizations comprised of a balance of energies, personalities, and body types. The working group, under the direction of an established teacher, provides access to realms of consciousness that may not be available to any of the members individually. Whether you are working alone, with a teacher, or with a group, you may find the group guidelines essential to understand the levels of consciousness within the great circle of consciousness.

GUIDELINES FOR GROUPS

The Teacher

The ideal situation is for all groups to be formed by a true master. However, this seldom is the case. An accomplished meditation teacher becomes frustrated with beginners, preferring to do the advanced spiritual work of evolving consciousness. Therefore, most groups are begun by aspiring initiates. In my own organization, I have developed a certification program for teachers in order to establish a minimum level of competence. Some of these teachers are not impressive, perhaps not verbal, and maybe not even very good people, but they have a gift. This gift should not be confused with the gifts of healing, psychic insights, prescience, and so on. The true gift of teachers is that their qualities advance your own essence.

In selecting a teacher, don't be blinded by the phenomena a person can produce. Apply the same amount of scrutiny in selecting a teacher that you would in buying a house. Test your inclination. Don't rely on blind faith, stated lineages from established traditions, or the recommendations of others. Cross-check everything, and if a vital element is discovered, then that teacher is on to something real. The student is risking life and soul in this work and must use great discernment in the selection of a teacher. However, do not fall into the trap of waiting for the perfect teacher. It is better to risk making a mistake than to never begin at all. Even as you begin, prepare for the realization that this may be a miss-start. You may have to start over with a different teacher or even a different system.

On the other hand, be careful not to abandon a teacher just because the process hurts. Hurt may be your personal pride or your ego's way of persuading you that this kind of transformative work should not be done. Therefore, start over only when it is too easy or you are not growing. Frequently, the human psyche needs to hurt badly enough before it is willing to change. However, abuse is not to be tolerated. If there is a true relationship between student and teacher, there is a compassion and zeal for self-discovery that overrides the pointing out of truths you may not wish to confront.

Ultimately, it will take several exposures to the real teaching essence before you realize that you have hooked into a teaching tradition. Fundamentally, all teachers provide the same function. They initiate you into higher awareness. Whether the subject matter is metaphysics, art, cooking, or rock-climbing, they transmit a higher consciousness through their interactions. You are not just attending a workshop, you are forming a relationship.

The Teacher-Student Relationship

Suppose, however, that you desire to start your own meditation group. Be aware that the rewards and frustrations eventually balance out, but initially, you may find the greatest challenge is just to keep a group together. For most people, the desire to meditate isn't enough to overcome their own inertia. It's just too easy to stay at home and watch television. The group leader must find ways to stimulate interest in the group. According to the leader's skills, there can be demonstrations of high energy levels, or guided shamanic journeys, or basic energy sensing or healing skills. Once the level of fascination convinces people that something worthwhile is happening, more traditional meditation work can be taught. The initial task for the beginning teacher, though, is to find a way to attract and maintain a group.

No one benefits more from the group than the beginning teacher. The teacher becomes the object of group members' ego projections. These reflections allow the teacher to uncover inner strengths, weaknesses, and flaws. During this difficult and sometimes terribly confrontative process, the most valuable words a teacher can offer are "I don't know" or "I am working on it." A scrupulous honesty will prevent a lot of heartache and mistrust down the road. The group dynamics, levels of energy, and the scarcity of real teachings may lead a talented beginning teacher beyond his or her abilities. Therefore, the tutelage of a mentor may prove invaluable.

At some time, a leader will be faced with criticism of the chosen leadership style. If you set the premise that all criticism be discussed in the group face-to-face, you will find that conflicts are more easily resolved. Gossip has no place in the workings of a spiritual group. I define gossip as when the subject of the conversation turns from the two people engaged in it to an absent third party. Clarity and honesty are the mainstays of a good working meditation group.

The formation of a working group is not a democracy, but a benevolent dictatorship. Invariably some students will leave the group no matter what the leader does or does not do. Though departures are best done in a high, clear, conscious space, occasionally there are highly charged dynamics surrounding the member. The group may struggle through this change and growth will be necessary on everyone's part. Any one teacher is not right for everyone, and a teacher should not encourage or discourage people from leaving. In many instances, when students leave for ego conflicts, they resolve their issues and return when it is appropriate. These dynamic events keep the group from suffering boredom!

The accomplished teacher will find it more difficult to be motivated with the simple work and creative games that attract novices to a working meditation group, yet the more sophisticated students sense the teacher's inner radiance, and that alone will be more than enough to attract and maintain them as students. If your inner identity is maintained, the dynamics of the group will flow around the teacher. Ultimately, free will and freedom of choice dictate any student's participation in a working group.

That is not to say that the teacher or master doesn't use games, clever phrases, or additions of higher energies to bring the group to attention. The master conducts the symphony of energies within the working group. Once the group is engaged at its higher level of consciousness, the teacher's own radiance increases immensely. Imagine this process as a pair of mirrors with light bouncing between them. Each reflection enhances the other. Both the teacher and the student are enormously advanced in clarity and luminosity.

The relationship between student and teacher is not one based on comfort. The real goal is to assist the student to break free of old patterns while being sustained in spiritual nourishment. A teacher uses many tactics to bring change. Don't get caught up in the teacher's personality, appearance, or words. His or her inner identity changes patterns according to the receiving ability of the student. The student-teacher relationship is extremely intimate and personalized. Direct comparisons with others' experiences may become a detriment to personal growth. A friend and I shared totally different experiences with the same teacher. At times, I was jealous of my friend's ability to have a simple casual conversation with our teacher. Of course, this emotional experience provided a fertile ground to work out my own ego issues. Self-reflection on the interactions of the group and teacher will teach you much. For a smoother journey, allow the energy to come through the teacher, incorporate it, and then transcend it. Don't crystallize or stagnate in your own pattern. The student-teacher relationship is about change and transformation.

Ultimately, you are responsible for your own spiritual practice and the connection to the teacher. The relationship will be fresh, vibrant, and spirited. The underlying dynamic is a sense of duty. The spiritual seeker's hunger is combined with the discipline of applied work to achieve higher consciousness. There is the willingness and commitment to the necessary work. This duty is not just intellectual or even contractual—there is also a warrior aspect. The sense of duty cannot be created or given, but comes from deep longings within the student.

Both student and teacher strive for knowing versus understanding. The relationship over time develops specialized meanings for what appears to others as ordinary events. A simple word may invoke a memory in a highly charged ritual, or a shared moment in a transcendent space. While most Americans have only one word for snow, the native Alaskans have a multitude of words that define the subtleties of the different types of snow. The goal is to have the experience of the various types of snow instead of just knowing what the different words mean.

The student's duty lies not just with the teacher, but also with the self, and with the group of seekers with which he or she associates. While the teacher always hopes for group members motivated by burning questions, desires, or needs, members arrive with a variety of motivations. Those students who become initiates all share the trait of inquisitive self-examination. While the teacher reflects back to them issues that need examination, the responsibility for being conscious and growing remains with the students. Initiates are spiritual seekers who capitalize on the opportunities for growth.

Though all initiates constantly scrutinize themselves, make sure that self-examination does not turn into judgment. Consider yourself as a scientist observing a laboratory animal. You may observe the action, make note of it, and decide whether or not that act should and could be changed, then you act accordingly. Ideally, there is no guilt or self-reproach involved.

EXERCISE I

This exercise works best after you have meditated and are in a relatively clear, quiet space. Take a deep breath and allow yourself to remember a conflict where you felt anger, guilt, or shame arise. Whether it was an argument with your spouse, yelling at your children, or being chastised by your boss, allow the dynamic to play out in your mind. Attempt to remain a passive observer as the scene evolves. Keep breathing deeply. Observe yourself objectively.

Then, take a few more deep breaths and allow the scene to fade away. When you have found that clear, quiet space again, let the conflict emerge and observe the actions, this time from another's perspective. Breathe deeply and sense the emotions, fears, and pain from the other's point of view. Take a deep breath and review the dynamics until the end. Then use a few deep breaths to clear this from your mind.

Continue this process until you have experienced everyone's role in this interaction. If guilt or shame arise, take a deep breath, and when you exhale, release these feelings. They do not serve you and frequently consume your physical, emotional, and mental energy. Strive to accept your actions, and realize that you did the best you could with what you knew at that time. With self-examination invoking personal growth, you have the power to change. Faced with similar circumstances again, you have the choice to change how you would handle the situation.

EXERCISE 2

Write or record your telling of the entire story of a conflict. Note the surroundings, how you felt, what emotions ran through you, and how the dynamics progressed. Put as much detail as you can remember into it. Set it aside for a few minutes, hours, or days. The waiting period varies according to the amount of "charge" or stored energy the story requires to sustain.

Now, write or tell the whole story again without referring to your original account. Summon the details of your conflict. Recreate the dynamics again. Incorporate the conversations, the tone of voice, the details of your surroundings, and your feelings before and after this occurrence. When you are finished, let the story rest.

Keep repeating the writing or recording process until there is no longer any emotional, physical, or mental reaction contained in the process of writing your account. The story will lose its charge. Then, and only then, go back and read the various accounts you generated. Look for subtle changes in your story. Did one version make you look better than in another account? Which parties held the most anger? How would you change the dynamics if you could? A careful reflection on these accounts will teach you a lot about the inner nature of your psyche.

True seekers consistently seek to remain conscious of higher realms while engaged in daily routines. Throughout the day, they strive to be conscious for short intervals. Even when you are working alone, you may do exercises to help you remain conscious.

EXERCISE 3

Convert a habit in such a way as to remind you to be more conscious. Select something that you do on a regular basis, such as looking at your watch, turning on the television, or emptying the trash. Place a peel-off sticker on the object to provide you with a visual reminder to breathe deeply, to notice the body and its senses, and to experience fully the higher awareness while engaged in mundane reality. You are learning to meditate while doing everyday tasks.

EXERCISE 4

Wear a loose rubberband around your wrist. Whenever someone comments on it or it otherwise attracts your attention, instead of reacting immediately, take a moment to breathe deeply, center your awareness, and then respond. Notice how differently you feel in this interaction.

EXERCISE 5

Place a Post-It note with a favorite quotation or word on your computer or refrigerator. You might write down a quality that you wish to embrace more fully, such as peace, compassion, gratitude, or love, or incorporate a favorite quotation for consideration, for example, "Unity is in a dance with the duality of reality," "I am a work in process," or "Life is a journey, not a destination."

Each time you approach these objects, you connect with the thoughts representing qualities or values that you wish to bring into your life.

A student of mine placed a peel-off label with the design of a bee on it over his watch. Every time he glanced at his watch to look at the time, there was a "Be" reflecting back to him. This simple reminder is a metaphor for the larger constant struggle to build a true identity. The frequent short intervals are more effective than long sessions. Compare this to doing sit-ups. The daily struggle of doing ten sit-ups per day is more effective than attempting to make up for a week's skipped exercises on Saturday by attempting to do seventy sit-ups.

EXERCISE 6

Examine your resistance to change by making a list of your top ten pet peeves. Include such things as, "I can't stand anyone telling me what to do," or "I don't like the green color of that new drink so I'm not going to try it." Make the list quickly, as the first few items to surface will later be more helpful.

After you complete the list, look for any patterns. Are there any issues of control showing through? Are there patterns of doubt or of doing the right thing? Perhaps there are issues of jealousy or insecurity? Look at your resistance to actually performing these exercises. Maybe there are issues around joining a group. Examine these pet peeves as reflections of issues within yourself. Be gentle and nonjudgmental with this process. No one knows you better than you. If you identify patterns that you would like to change, the first step is to recognize them, then you may bring more awareness and attention to them when they do arise. Finally, don't punish yourself if you are not able to change existing patterns immediately. With regular practice, you will find it easier. If you practice this in a highly conscious working group, then the change will be expedited, as the group will undoubtedly point out your issues.

MEMBERS' OBLIGATIONS TO THE GROUP

Within any established spiritual group, there is a harmony of exercises, energy, and meetings. If people do not use the tools, exercises, texts, and teachings, they cease to exist. The interplay between members and the teachings are critical for the continuance of higher consciousness within the members. To be alive, the group must change as the group vision evolves. In most groups of forty to fifty people, there are perhaps ten who do the work regularly, which, of course, creates an imbalance. The normal reaction is to say, "Well, that may be true of others, but not me. I am one of those ten." Be careful of the subtle ways you may deceive yourself. There are always ways to improve, even if you are one of those ten people. You don't make spiritual advances by winging it. Hard work is required to advance on the spiritual path. Your hunger can only be fed by self-discipline. You can't wait for your partner to catch up. You can't wait for your worldly work to be less involved because it might never be. You can't wait until next week, for it might not come. The spiritual work becomes an integral part of your life.

The duty to the group is more than showing up for a meeting. You must be an active participant. In addition to struggling to stay conscious and awake, you may take on organizational duties. At times, you will be the focus of someone else's process. Ultimately, becoming a vital part of a group reflects the same process of becoming a functional member of society. Be involved. Be concerned. Share from your place of truth as your inner sense of duty dictates. Group members form a part of a larger single functional being. Each person plays a part in maintaining the whole.

SELECTING GROUP MEMBERS

When you are first forming a working group, members may simply select themselves by showing up. However, as you gain experience you will look for various types, whether archetypal families, personalities, or physical body types, to include a broad cross-section of society. While you may think it is easier to select those with similar interests, the group may go stale rather quickly. New members who least resemble the teacher provide perspectives that might otherwise go unseen. At the same time, you must create a group that is able to harmonize. Traditionally, the needs of the group outweigh the needs of the individuals.

The dynamics of being in a group are stressful for teacher and members alike. From the beginning, you must strive to be professional in all interactions. The leader evaluates members' motivations, commitments, skills, and desires. While there is a certain amount of social interaction to accommodate the group, this should not be the primary motivation. The goal is to interact and learn, and you should find threads of commonality to keep the group moving forward. A mission statement that clearly defines the reason for the group's existence keeps the meetings on track.

For many newcomers to the work, the ability to make a commitment will be extremely difficult. Since the process of transformation is so demanding, some students are unable to subject their pride and ego to group dynamics. Only a commitment to the group carries them across their personal challenges. One way to build the ability to commit is to require relatively short duration commitments. For example, the first commitment may be for only a series of six meetings. At the end of that time, the group and the teacher may reassess their goals. Announce early in the forming of a group process that there is an evaluation after each commitment interval. For some, the notice itself increases stress levels, yet this reevaluation is important to both student and teacher, and should become an accepted part of the process.

The most endearing quality for any group member is the innate hunger to know and explore the self and the universe. The sharing of an expanded awareness or the uncovering of hidden talents creates an overwhelming joy. With enough of these small enlightenments, the challenges of being in a group will be overcome.

The beginning teacher and new groups will make many mistakes. The selection and rejection of students will provide experience in forming a balanced working circle. If you have the internal strength, inner hungers, and a high level of commitment, the formation of a dynamic group is a great learning process.

Groups fall into patterns—both supportive and destructive. However, being too familiar or too predictable means that the group has reached an end. You can bring in more new people to break up existing patterns. I have always been opposed to the same people meeting for years at a time. There should be an ebb and flow of members within the group, otherwise there is stagnation. This group exists because of the leader's efforts in providing constant growth and establishing a spiritual direction. Therefore, the responsibility lies with the leader to either end a group or change it significantly to keep it fresh and vital.

The point and focus of a conscious working group is to make a difference in the world. The meditation group must be involved and engaging in order to bring higher awareness to others. This is *not* a self-help group. This is *not* a get-together, feel-good group. This is *not* a coven. This is more. Transformative meditation groups are about relationships as a way to enlightenment and transcendence.

MEETING GUIDELINES

Groups must establish a reason to meet; you as the leader must establish an intent. Normally, the leader is the coordinator of place, time, and frequency. Initially, you must establish these guidelines without trying to obtain group consensus, otherwise the group will be frustrated. The initial commitment is made when you dictate the first meeting and outline the structure for the first working period. It is much easier to establish strict guidelines at first and then loosen them than it is to put discipline into an unstructured group.

Meetings should be held regularly at first. Human beings are creatures of habit and will find it more convenient to attend if the meetings are held at the same time and place each week. Other intervals are possible, but the initial commitment should be short. In meeting weekly, the memory of previous work can be retained more easily.

Punctuality is an expression of mindfulness. Meetings should begin and end on time. If there is work that may extend past the allotted time, a proven tactic is to request the group's permission for an extension or to end formally on time, but for those who wish to continue, they may remain for another few minutes. In this way, you honor the time commitments and the energetic process.

Meetings are generally opened with a formal or silent connection to your own group and teacher. For my own groups, I created an invocation that you may use as well:

We are a circle of seekers,
United by our quest to evolve, transcend, and know.
We honor those who traveled before us
And continue to light the path for those who follow.

The transformative techniques you learn are the result of many who have made the journey ahead of you. Honor all those who traverse the path. If you are working with a mentor, you may establish a connection to allow the higher energetic connection to flow through you.

With the intent set with the invocation, ensure that the meeting place is comfortable and convenient. There are some advantages to meeting in the same place each time, as doing so instills a familiarity and expectation. Energies of transformation are stored in the furnishings and reminders of the room. That same expectation may also be disadvantageous, as people begin to habituate to the meetings and may find it harder to embrace change.

Pay attention to how you arrange the seats or floor pillows as well. Many teachers have the group sit in a circle, since a circle is a symbol of spirit and continuity. Additionally, sitting in a circle promotes equality of membership, as even the teacher is just another link in the chain. Different seating patterns, such as the square or parabola, can be tried to determine how each pattern affects the group's energy. Archetypal patterns have different results.

Pay attention to the room's aesthetics. As a focus, you may choose to place a lit candle in the center of the circle. Be sure to use a tray underneath it in case it is overturned. The use of incense, lit before the meeting, may leave a lingering scent in the room. Some people are allergic, so use caution when burning any fragrance during meetings. Bright lights seem intrusive when reopening your eyes after meditation, so dim lights when possible. My personal meditation space uses simple rope lighting around the perimeter of the ceiling, which gives a soft, muted light. The use of natural products such as wood, stone, and plants enhance the room's ability to hold higher energies.

Last, but not least, establish calling trees for the group. In emergencies, meetings may have to be cancelled unexpectedly. Calling trees that have one or two members, who in turn notify one or two members, save a lot of time in conveying messages. The group also begins to take responsibility from within. Ultimately, you will find that the attempt to create a group is a great learning experience all by itself. The work of spiritual enlightenment, and perhaps transcendence, is extremely difficult, while the rewards are tremendous.

> All the world's a stage,
> And all the men and women merely players
> They have their exits and their entrances.
> And one man in his time plays many parts
> His acts being seven stages. At first the infant,
> mewling and puking in the nurse's arms,
> Then the whining schoolboy with his satchel
> And shining morning face, creeping like snail
> Unwillingly to school. And then the lover,
> Sighing like furnace, with a woeful ballad
> made to his mistress' eyebrow. Then, a soldier,
> Full of strange oaths, and bearded like the pard
> Jealous in honor, sudden and quick in quarrel,
> Seeking the bubble reputation
> even in the cannon's mouth. And then the justice
> in fair round belly with good capon linded
> With eyes severe and beard of formal cut.
> Full of wise saws and modern instances;
> And so he plays his part. The sixth age shifts
> into the lean and slippered pantaloon,
> With spectacles on nose and pouch on side,
> His youthful hose, well saved; a world too wide
> For his shrunk shank, and his big manly voice,
> Turning again toward childish treble, pipes
> And whistles in his sound. Last scene of all,

That ends this strange, eventful history,
Is second childishness and mere oblivion,
Sans teeth, sans eye, sans taste, sans everything.

—Shakespeare, *As You Like It*

Shakespeare's *As You Like It* excerpt provides a rich and descriptive view of life. You can also skim over this excerpt and simply categorize it as "That's life." In a richer view, the excerpt defines the qualities, experiences, and processes of life. By delineating the whole, the segments are seen and experienced more fully. The timeless quality of the whole is realized with others through the utilization of shared time and space. Life can now be experienced as a tangible quality, yet life retains its wholeness as well. The paradox of time and timelessness is a mirror to that of life and death.

Similarly, the process of meditation when examined on multiple levels reveals the richness of reality in a different way. Each progressive level contains a universal quality that can be detected by various means. Just as it is possible to sense the outer world by sight, sound, sensation, and so on, it is possible to examine many meditation levels easily by intuition, clairvoyance, kinesthetic feeling, detection of light, and vibration or sound intensity. These are qualities that everyone has to some degree, but we have not been taught to use them. In fact, you may have been taught that these levels and abilities are not real, and that you should not pay attention to them. Remember to keep an open mind to possibility.

For example, when you come out of a meditation, the air may seem thicker. The atmosphere may seem to be vibrating slower or faster. You may also perceive different qualities of light, such as different colors, intensities, and patterns. The presence, absence, and quality of light provide easily identifiable markers for specific levels of meditation; however, if you do not see light, it is not necessarily a handicap. In fact, finding the "higher" spaces that don't have light is easier if you are not preoccupied with detecting light. Other modes of detection such as sensation, density, or richness are subtler, but are far less likely to deceive. The most important aspect of identifying levels is to examine the self for a noticeable change when a new level is entered. Through many years of leading groups through this progression, there is proven uniformity of the experiences at each defined level. Often a teacher takes a meditation group into a new realm and asks for comparisons; after enough introductions, members of a group can accurately detect changes in their perceptions.

Chapter Five

THE TRANSFORMATIVE
MEDITATION LEVELS

PHYSICAL AND ETHERIC LAYER

You should have a solid, healthy foundation before embarking on a journey into higher awareness. As you progress on your metaphysical journey, you will encounter events that will challenge you on every front. Assuming that you're ready, let's begin with the physical layer, which most people experience with sensory awareness as "everyday waking reality." The physical plane can also be defined in the Buddhists' terms as "matter with sentience," and "the capability of feeling." This becomes important when you consider the role of the Bodhisattva, a being who postpones transcendence of this plane until all sentient beings achieve enlightenment. If all matter is sentient, there is a lot of work to be done in bringing planetary enlightenment.

In my own transformation system, I do consider all matter to hold some form of consciousness, as I explained during a graduate school presentation on consciousness. Since many professors found my seminars provoking, but not in traditional academic form, there was little discussion until my major professor asked if a copy machine has consciousness. This caught me by surprise; I paused, and then reached for a higher clarity to form an answer. I began a short exposition on the nature of quantum mechanics, explaining that consciousness and form are interdependent. "The act of observing form determines an object. If consciousness determines the very form of any object," I concluded, "and atoms must hold some conscious awareness, then a Xerox machine, comprised of atoms, must have some form of consciousness."

For most people, however, the spiritual transformation work begins with the self. Defining the physical layer is much easier from that perspective; the physical is defined as that which is tangible. Even in its simplicity, this definition differs subtly according to the sensitivities of individuals. What you limit to the physical realm, others see as the closest layer, or the etheric layer. These artificially defined realms of the physical and etheric on the step pyramid style meditation map are also interpenetrating. However, the distinction serves a pedagogic use to allow conscious exploration of subtleties that are frequently lost by only viewing the whole.

The energy that maintains the physical form and radiates out slightly beyond that form is the etheric layer. This realm defines the manifestation of the physical body from its astral blueprint, and is also the beginning of the metaphysical realm for most. However, the etheric layer can be photographed with Kirlian photography, and can be detected in other ways. Clairvoyants, with their vision beyond normal human capabilities, see a shadowy glow or fuzziness at the edges of the physical form. Other sensitive people can detect the etheric layer as waves of heat or vibration. Likewise, some healers and body workers ably detect etheric energies and add or extract energy from this realm. Small changes on the etheric layer greatly affect the physical realm because the etheric layer interacts directly between the physical body and the astral energies. This is the basic principle underlying most healing techniques.

GROUP EXERCISE I: VISUALLY SENSING AND DETECTING THE ETHERIC REALMS

1. Invoke your personal connection to a higher awareness, or, meditate to find a clear, empty awareness.

2. Find a partner to sit facing you for this exercise, or if you're working alone, sit in front of a mirror.

3. Make sure that your partner sits in front of a white or light colored wall or that your reflection contrasts against a plain background.

4. Gaze at the person or reflection in the same way you look out over the ocean. This utilizes the soft focus mode that allows you to take in long distances. When used to see close-up objects, you use your vision to see in an unconventional way.

5. Holding this soft focus, just allow the image to shimmer or lose its hard edges. For example, as I gazed at my friend's face, I noticed in my peripheral vision that her arm glowed in a white light that surrounded it. This fuzziness was perhaps only an inch or two away from the physical boundary of her body.

6. Try this exercise several times and note any changes in perception. (Take care not to strain your eyes by staring too long at anything.)

GROUP EXERCISE 2: SENSING THE ETHERIC AND ASTRAL REALMS

1. Meditate to find an empty clarity. If you are working with a group or teacher, invoke your connection to either. This exercise yields the best results when you work with a partner who can give you verbal feedback, but you can also practice sensing the etheric realm with a pet or even a houseplant. For simplicity, I'll assume you'll be working with a female partner.

2. Have your partner stand in the middle of the room. Make sure that there is space to move freely around her.

3. Ask her to close her eyes and to inform you if she feels where your hand is sensing.

4. Then, using your nondominant hand (if you're right-handed, use your left hand and vice versa), allow the hand to sense the energy emanating from your partner. Approach her back with your hand extended at heart level. When you detect a pressure, vibratory, or

heat change, explore the edges of that field by moving your hand slowly around her body without touching her.

5. Continue to explore the edges of this field by moving around your partner's body and head.

6. Share your results with your partner and offer to reverse roles.

INTRODUCTION TO THE FORMATION AND USE OF ENERGY CIRCLES

The human body has great ability to consciously span many vibratory levels. All levels coexist and interpenetrate. As you've seen from the previous exercises, they can sensitize you to detecting energy with the hands and soft-focused vision. Just as a room is filled with air, heat waves, TV and radio signals, and other energies beyond our detection, the lower and upper astral—as well as all the higher realms of consciousness—co-occupy the space. All vibratory levels exist simultaneously, and all fields interpenetrate. The job of learning to distinguish and operate them means becoming a "proper receiver." The discipline of progressive meditation is to pick your way through these fields with a qualified teacher who animates one particular field of vibration. When you can detect that vibration, that level is achieved and "marked" in your consciousness. Later, when you encounter the same marker, whether it is light, a feeling, or a sensation, you can associate it with that level of consciousness.

The most effective method to explore higher realms of consciousness is through the use of energy circles. By forming a select group of people to combine strengths and weaknesses, you have more opportunity to directly experience a realm you might not have been able to on your own. For example, when my teacher entered a specific higher realm of consciousness that I wasn't quite ready for, my stomach became upset. My body was giving me a marker that assisted in identifying my progress. From then on in meditation, I knew that when my stomach became upset, we were entering that realm. With enough forays and experience in that realm, my stomach problems disappeared. I learned to recognize that level of consciousness in other ways, and was able to acquire and integrate the information of that realm. At that point, my inner identity was strong enough to function fully in both realms of consciousness.

THE ROLE OF EGO AND PERSONALITY IN GROUP CIRCLE WORK

Energy circles assist in introducing higher awareness while group members may still be individually resolving ego and personality issues. Most schools of thought on the transformation process include much information on the role of ego, but tend to be confusing and contradictory with each other. In transformational meditation work, a student must have a strong, healthy ego. People with a weak ego are probably not good candidates for group transformative meditation work, as they are prone to be easily affected by random forces outside their own. At the same time, potential members must have enough confidence to be flexible enough to shed their egoic boundaries and merge into the group. This state of a healthy ego is necessary for the formation of true will—the ability to manifest what you consciously desire and are. Part of the group work is to assist willing individuals to develop a healthy ego, but the circle should not develop into a self-help group. The goal of achieving higher awareness and evolving consciousness remains the focus of a working meditation group.

Distinction between personality and ego strength is very important. You can easily live without personality, but ego strength is vital. Ego development begins with the recognition of your separateness in response to your survival instinct. It is critical for you to recognize the needs of your body and to have them met. The ego ensures the survival of the body and serves as a structure that supports true identity. Ego can be converted to a higher process of being—frequently through a near-death experience or through an initiation. Both initiation and near-death experiences catalyze such major transformations in mind, body, and spirit that the event in many ways equates to death, except the physical body survives. A strong, healthy ego is necessary to be willing to face dying. At times of great pain or when facing the possibility of death, personality and any associated neuroses disappear. You become much clearer regarding the essentials of life.

Transformative meditation offers a more subtle initiation into transcending personal egos. To overcome the issues of ego, personal space, and personal pride, standing energy transmission circles may be used. It is impossible to stand in a group, participate in what is happening, and remain aloof and isolated. The circle acts as a chain with individuals as links. If someone doesn't interact with the circle, nothing happens, since the chain is broken. Each participant must release the personal barriers to allow energy to flow around the circle. This flow of energy is often felt as pleasurable, warm, or tingly. For the individuals who are not interacting or are in some way resistant to lowering personal boundaries, they will be wondering why others are smiling or having these great experiences. Again, the feeling of individual "me-ness" or separateness must be released. The paradox is that you must maintain boundaries to be able to stand within the group for anything to happen, but at the same time, you must let go of the feeling that it is private space. Privacy is an illusion. The body is porous and is constantly subjected to multitudes of energy emanations. Simply consider beyond the sun's rays the enormous amount of energy transmitted through space—cellular phone calls, television or radio signals, heat, love, or thought. All these emanations are available at all times. It is only a matter of tuning in to them with an appropriate receiver to be aware of and to interact with them. Collective meditation is one way to create such a receiver.

The human body and mind comprise an extremely complicated receiver made up of very little solid material and mostly empty space. A field of consciousness electromagnetically holds the pattern that allows the space and material to become form. Realize that your own energy radiates out to the environment as well as being permeable to other types of energy. The ego serves as a filter to other types of energy to ensure that its pattern is not destroyed or damaged. The ego is fulfilling its duty to ensure the survival of the body. Since many of these filters and defenses are developed in childhood or infancy, many of the egoic energy filters have lived long past their useful life. They now prevent the awarenesses and feelings that may lead to the knowing of true reality. These energy filters that have protected us for so long must now be unraveled. This is the true work of developing a healthy, strong ego. A teacher or mystic is able to read these energetic filters and determine a student's state of development. For such advanced mystics and some clairvoyants, these energetic emanations from the body are easily read.

When individuals combine their energy emanations in a group circle, a safe space must be created where the individuals may experiment with the removal of these filters that produce the illusion of separateness. This temporary experience allows them to build confidence in their ability to be without their normal defense mechanisms. Peer pressure and a quick read of everyone's mental, emotive, and energy state will overcome ego objections and the circle will form.

When standing in an energy circle, you may not be informed of the multidimensional aspects of the circle's use. Everyone experiences shifts in consciousness in a unique way. Others sharing the same circle may have entirely different experiences from you. Discussions among participants afterward often bring out the various aspects. Let experiences be the teaching and let the sharing provide perspectives.

GROUP EXERCISE 3: DISTINGUISHING ENERGIES WITHIN THE GROUP

1. As in all exercises, use your group invocation or meditate for group clarity before beginning an exercise.

2. Have the group pair off with a partner. Using the guidelines of Group Exercise 2 (page 93), have each pair sense each other's energy and provide feedback. You may wish to time this exercise so that everyone finishes at approximately the same time.

3. Ask the group to form a circle, and make sure partners are not standing next to each other. Ask them to stand with their feet shoulder-width apart, their knees bent, and their eyes closed. This position is a very stable, balanced posture.

4. Ask the members to join hands loosely, keeping their right palm facing down and their left hand up. Ask them to refrain from talking unless they have a question about your instructions.

5. Now, instruct them to send out energy through their right hand and allow the left hand to receive energy from the person next to them. Give this a few moments, as it will be new for a lot of people and reflected in nervous laughter or uncertainty. Be patient.

6. Ask the members to nod if they feel energy in the circle. If you see that several people do not nod, you can ask that the circle increase the amount of energy sent, or ask them to simply imagine that they do feel energy. Some people will report heat or other physical sensations, and you can suggest that they focus on passing the energy through them.

7. Ask the group members to continue to keep their eyes closed, but as they send out energy request that they locate their partner by his or her energy. When they have done so, have them imagine an inner vision of their circle and the location of their partner.

8. Have everyone open their eyes and compare their inner vision with the real composition of the circle. Discuss how the experiment affected them.

ESTABLISHING VOCABULARY

The sharing of the individuals' experiences serves many purposes, including bonding, providing different perspectives, and learning to articulate energetic information. This latter exercise leads to the development of a common group vocabulary. Indeed, this is one of the most important reasons for asking for feedback from the group.

In a standing energy circle, you may select certain energies to transmit to the group. For example, send a simple grounding energy to the circle and ask people to give their reactions or sensory awareness. Recognize that one mode of learning is to relate something unknown to something known. Many people will first find a reactive body response such as heat, chills, pressure in the head, and so on. Encouraging all responses, you establish that the most important point of the standing circle is to be noting changes. There may be a surprising correlation or disparity with participants' responses. There are no wrong answers. Some members will find a confirmation between the teacher's invocation and their experience helpful while others will find the disparity distressing. Once the circle understands this process, you build a common vocabulary by changing the energies transmitted and asking for feedback. Provide enough variations of energy transmissions to develop the sensitivity and recognition of energy for the group.

GROUP EXERCISE 4: SENSING ENERGY THROUGH INNER VISION

1. The first step is to ensure that the group begins with clarity—either through meditation or an invocation.

2. Ask the group to form a circle and have the members stand with their feet shoulder-width apart, their knees bent, and their eyes closed.

3. Ask the members to join hands loosely, keeping their right palm facing down and their left hand up. Remind them to refrain from talking unless they have a question about your instructions.

4. Now, instruct them to feel their connection to the earth beneath them. Visualize the energy of the earth rising up through the legs and from its great reservoir, filling the body with its energy. Maintain this stage until most people seem to be energized and/or growing warm.

5. Next, have them send out this excess energy through their right hand and allow the left hand to receive energy from the person next to them. Give this a few moments, as it will be new for a lot of people and reflected in nervous laughter or uncertainty. Be patient.

6. As the group grows comfortable standing together holding hands, here are some experiments for you to try.

   • Send energy clockwise through the hands held around the circle.

   • Send energy counterclockwise through the hands in the circle.

   • Circulate energy though the various chakra levels.

   • Provide a grounding central force.

7. End the exercise by giving a quick squeeze to the hands you are holding, then disconnect. If the group exercise is successful, then the adjoining members will automatically do the same and drop their adjoining hands. The process should continue until the circle is broken. It is not unusual to have to coach the first group you work with.

Group members' responses usually provide physical clues to the energetic levels they are individually and collectively experiencing. Often these physical sensations are more valid than anything that can be said intellectually. The direct perception of these energy levels defined by physical reactions allows individuals to return to these states simply by recalling them. Memory allows for the recalling of the experience versus the recreation of the path to it. For example, if the group has expressed the sensation of being pulled upward or rising, the simple reminder of that sensation may invoke that same level of energy. Indeed, that is one of the secrets behind the true use of ritual. The physical reminder through symbol, chant, or movement may invoke the state of consciousness used to create it.

Physical clues also provide understanding as to how the body may incorporate more spiritual insight into its everyday awareness. Body experiences, such as the tension of muscles, the movement of the glottis during breathing, the position of the torso, arms, fingers, and so on, all mark and remember the awareness of a specific state of energy. As an experiment, meditate in different formations, positions, or movements, and discover different mudras that are significant. You might remember the experiences of these beginning exercises in observing posture. It is impossible to adequately describe what is felt during energy circles. If it is not remembered, then it might as well have never happened. If you can remember, you will eventually become conscious. While everyone has numerous mystical insights and flashes that range from a fraction of a second to a minute or two, only conscious people are able to remember them. They then begin to link these precious moments like pearls on a string. Eventually, they form a complete strand, and they almost continuously remain conscious.

GROUP EXERCISE 5: THE MECHANICS OF FORMING AN ENERGY CIRCLE

If your initial energy circles have been successful, you may wish to know more about the formal incorporation of a working circle. Here are more detailed instructions to use when you have established a circle with willing members.

1. To form an energy circle, have the participants stand in a circle with their feet shoulder-width apart. Their knees should be slightly bent and not in a locked position. Spacing between people should be sufficient to allow comfortable reaching to hold hands. Be mindful of height differences so that arms are not stretched at uncomfortable levels.

2. The holding of hands to form a continuous link in the circle is done in a specific way using the pattern of right hand palm down, left hand palm up. One of my students remembers this by using the pun "Write it down." The use of this pattern is to achieve a balance throughout the circle and to prevent all the aggressive people from pointing their hands down and of all the accepting people

from putting their palms up. Ensure that people make contact through the palms, since those are minor, but very sensitive, chakras for energy flow.

3. Another consideration for your circle formation is that it should be balanced. The men and women should be interspersed to take advantage of the natural polarity and charge of the opposite sexes. Couples should also be encouraged not to stand by each other, since their energy may be compatible enough together to be indistinguishable as two separate individuals.

4. Now the group may be challenged to sense the circle's balance. Just as the individuals used their own sensing abilities to locate their earlier exercise partner, now ask them to send their energy to sense the energy, and to move accordingly to adjust it. However, this physical adjustment vanishes after a variable length of time; the circle will balance itself by internal adjustments.

5. Last, but not least, treat the circle as a sacred spiritual space. Ask participants to be mindful of the connection they have made. Should they need to break circle and leave, they should join the hands of the individuals on either side of them together in front of the individual's body. When those two hands make contact, the person in the middle may release hands and back out of the circle. To rejoin the circle, the person should touch the joined hands of the two individuals he or she wishes to stand between. They will release the bond as they establish contact and allow the outsider to step into the unbroken circle.

INTRODUCING THE AWARENESS OF HIGHER ENERGY LEVELS

Now that the circle is established, the real work of introducing the group to the various levels of awareness begins. You may remind the participants that if they stand as they usually do, and talk, think, or intellectualize, their palms will get sweaty, and they may feel pleasure, but not much else happens. Yet something does happen automatically when people are in physical contact. The act of standing together, rubbing shoulders, hugging, or any other kind of acceptable touch provides a break in the ordinary ego barriers around the psyche. Within a few moments, a person will begin to either dislike or, in a relatively few of the cases, be attracted to the person next to them. This attraction is not necessarily of a sexual origin; however, even if it is, it does not have to be a genital or body attraction. This attraction is a simple revelation that the individual energies have begun to merge together.

One universal principle is that any system that discovers something similar to it will include the new addition in its fundamental nature. Love exists for your fundamental nature. Anything that you can identify with can be loved. Body workers, healers, or teachers know that if you work on someone, there is a feeling of love and compassion for him or her. The similar energies of both client and participant are blended. In the circle, although the group may be experiencing emotional pleasure, the purpose of the energy circles is to develop awareness of other levels of being.

GROUP EXERCISE 6: CREATING A COLLECTIVE FOCUS

1. After a meeting or two has established a group focus, you may be ready for more adventures in consciousness. Remember, groups become stagnant by too much repetition. Be sure to start with group clarity or invocation to a higher identity.

2. This time when you transmit energy into the circle, request that the members look for a change in their state. For example, are they feeling heat or possibly getting taller? Do they feel a flow of anything through the circle? After several people have responded, go to the next step.

3. Remind the circle of how they used their connection with earth to build energy in their body. Have everyone build energy, and when

the group collective reaches the maximum it can hold, have the members direct the overflow into the center of the circle and slightly above their heads. (This resembles the pattern of a maypole with ribbons of energy extended to each individual.) Visualize the ribbons tied in the high center point before releasing the circle.

4. Remember the creation of this collective point. Doing so will help your next circle start at a higher level of consciousness.

A teacher consciously selects how to interact with the circle and seeks feedback from the participants. Typical responses begin with reactions of the body—there may be a feeling of heat, a state of relaxation, or a feeling of becoming large. Some may suggest that they feel something flowing out from the body and may feel the adjoining people more. A few may even suggest a flow or current moving around the circle. Remaining conscious of the power of suggestion when establishing a vocabulary, you should carefully select words and questions to use appropriately. For example, note the difference between the following two questions: "Do any of you feel heat moving through your hands?" versus "Do any of you notice a change in your perception of the circle?"

Some members will not feel anything in the circle, and they will feel peer pressure to offer some remarks. To alleviate or even forestall this situation, a reminder is given that not everyone will feel these subtle energies when first exposed to them in the circle. It may take several introductions to these minute changes in awareness before they will be able to detect changes. For those who do not have direct experience of the changes, suggest that they imagine, daydream, or visualize that something happened.

GROUP EXERCISE 7: BRIDGING ENERGIES

Once the circle has obtained a small but functional vocabulary, try this exercise.

1. Establish the working energy circle and ensure that everyone feels a part of the circle.

2. Now, ask the participants to remain in the energy flow of the circle while separating their palms by a few inches. Generally, it is best to recommend that the eyes be closed so that the intellect will not be focused on the hands. Often with less sensory input, many people think less. If some do not wish to close their eyes, suggest that they keep their eyes relaxed by looking at the floor or off into the distance.

3. Now the teacher repeats the same energetic exercises previously done when the people had been holding hands. Again, ask for feedback to determine if the same kind of sensations can still be observed. Some individuals may feel the connection stronger than in the connected circle. If the group is able to achieve this, then the realm of the etheric body energies is left and the group enters the astral, the layer of awareness just beyond the physical.

4. With this accomplishment, you can elect to expand the vocabulary of the group by again sending signals through this circle. One great example is the sending of a pulse or wave. A human being easily distinguishes an on/off sensation when the teacher pulses the flow of energy. If there are members who do not feel the pulse sensations, the teacher may add more personal chi to increase the amplitude of the energetic pulse.

5. Another alternative is to change the frequency of the transmission. This may include a difference in timing between pulses or a difference in the level of the energy being transmitted. Through experimentation, the energy transmission may be selected or tuned to harmonize with both students' and group's receptive capability. The act of changing frequency in the circle creates a charge. This same charge might be created by circulating energy through the group at the different chakra levels. While these may invoke the sensations unique to that chakra level, the beginning group will most likely be responding on the body level.

6. Suggest that the group imagine rings circulating through it at different points of the body. For example, ask the group to sense a

flow of energy at the heart level. Hopefully by this point, the group is beyond the power of suggestion and quickly creates a strong flow of energy. The teacher then adjusts the frequency of transmission and the energy flows at the level of the feet. The group may immediately sense a change and offer comments. Explain to the members that you are trying to establish two working rings simultaneously, and solicit comments. The awareness of the difference between the energies provides the electrical charge that the group detects in varying ways.

GROUP EXERCISE 8: GROUNDING

The concentration of energy at the level of the feet or ground serves another important purpose: grounding. People react quite differently to the experience of the awareness of unfamiliar energies. Some, particularly those who already have difficulty being grounded and focused in their body, may feel faint or become dizzy. By concentrating the energy at ground level, the teacher can, by grounding, bring the students fully into their body. For these select individuals, this brings about a richness and fullness of being fully embodied on this plane for the first time. Grounding may be required whenever the energy begins to overwhelm a person. The teacher always establishes a strong ground connection before beginning anything with a circle, and is prepared for immediate intervention for students.

While this multiple feedback process may seem tedious, it serves the important function of sensitizing the group and providing a common vocabulary. In doing so, there is a rudimentary foundation on which to build a group meditation.

GROUP EXERCISE 9: ALTERNATIVE CIRCLE FORMATION TECHNIQUE

1. The leader establishes the circle with the participants holding hands and uses either invocation or meditation to create clarity before beginning.

2. The leader then asks the individuals to feel their personal space in addition to feeling the weight that is connecting them to the earth. By first encouraging a feeling of personal space, the group can more easily feel the physical space between them and the person on either side of them. Realize that you are asking for a jump in awareness by noticing the space instead of the physical objects.

3. Now the group becomes aware of the adjoining individuals by feeling or sensing their presence. If the energy presence of the person can be detected, this is a clear indication that awareness is being brought to the ego shield that is primarily existent in the astral.

4. When most of the group has achieved this feeling, instruct the members of the circle to open their awareness to include the presence of others' energy. To reinforce the idea that no one will disappear into the group, a helpful metaphor is offered. Imagine that you become transparent to allow the energy to interpenetrate. Once the ego boundaries have been opened, you can enter every other person's individual space and vice versa. Emphasis is placed on the fact that everyone in the circle is neutral and safe. It is okay for you to enlarge through the body of the circle. Another reminder that may alleviate ego or boundary concerns is that there is already a connection established at the heart level. You can encourage an expansion sideways from your own personal space and see how many bodies can be moved through in both directions.

5. When the teacher and group both detect an energy flow, the group has passed a major threshold. The teacher senses the members of the group as a single organism, the circle itself. There is now a sense of unity; a single body of conscious energy exists.

Be careful of explanation at this point, as great gaps in this energy body can appear with the engagement of intellect. You must emphasize feeling, not intellectual understanding. Remind group members that their egos define a separate sense of self, and that an intellectual inquiry at this point may increase that isolation. The goal of a working circle is to transcend the ego level and become a single organism. Distinctions of self are not lost, but are now part of a familiar whole. The individuals merge into a larger identity that not only has a soul, but is also comprised of beloved friends, lovers, or family. With the recognition of a harmony among members that allows love to flow into the created circle, you can reexamine the sense of personal space. If the group has been lifted into a higher realm, you, along with several others, may report that your personal space feels extended beyond the physical space of the head.

The key element of this form of the standing energy circle is to feel the weight of the body on the floor as background while the participant begins to experience the sensation of being conscious at a level above the body and out of the top of the head. The particular quality of holding awareness at two points, above and below the head, is the desired result. Many students report feeling as if they are half in the body and half above it. This is a clear indication of the state of the lower astral. If you intuitively or clairvoyantly attempt to measure the extension of the students' bodies where the awareness is felt, perhaps two or three feet above the head, the circle seems to shrink slightly. This layering of energetic awareness resembles the tiers of Zoser's pyramid in Egypt, or even a wedding cake (see figure 3).

When the group is firmly established in the lower astral, you may automatically sense the others' innermost intentions. There are literally no secrets. Some people can be sweet and kind on the outside, but the openness of the lower astral group space may reveal that they are really cut off and not feeling. The overly aggressive personality may be seen as the facade for an inner shy person as well. The astral is a good place to begin knowing the inner motivation of each participant.

When you are observing this circle formation, be cautious of "heady" people—ones who live mostly in their mind, who don't have much grounding to work with from the beginning. If you greatly feel your connection to earth, you may need to share your personal space with them. Without grounding, some people may faint in the circle.

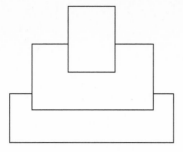

Figure 3: Layers of energetic awareness interpenetrate each other.

With too much grounding, you may not experience the higher, lighter vibratory realms. The sharing of energy among the circle members is important, and the teacher must constantly evaluate and balance the circle.

ILLUSIONS OF MOVEMENT

Many circle participants will report the sense of movement that is, of course, illusionary. While many may express a sensation of going up, in actuality you don't go anywhere. This illusion of movement occurs because you are simply changing the nature of what you are identifying with in the individual inner awareness. To relate back to the human being as a flexible receiver, you have simply changed the station and are now able to receive the programming on that level.

The sensation of movement upward (and no one to date has reported a downward trend) suggests a change in the agreement between body, ego, and mind. The body has recognized a shift or change in its receiver and is attempting to adjust as best as it can. The body, usually focused on such issues as weight and motion, is trying to incorporate issues of the psyche within the flesh. This interaction changes its normal association with gravity and makes the sensation of a rising movement. While the body views gravity as something that draws it earthward, consciousness, with its lesser mass, is not pulled as tightly. You might say it is similar to helium rising within a balloon.

Consequently, when you break out of the body's containment vibration, there is the sensation of rising.

TEACHERS AND TRANSFORMATIVE ENERGIES IN CIRCLE

A qualified and proven teacher is the only guarantee that the proper use of transformative energies within the circle will be done. Within this body of work, I certify teachers for three levels of work. The first level of certification is for those who can easily and safely create an integrated group energy within the astral. The second level requires that a teacher perform the sensitive transition out of the astral into the transpersonal or causal realms. The third certification, which few students attempt, is to span the entire spectrum of energy to transform self and others. Generally, a teacher is expected to have a fully integrated identity at the level beyond personal certification.

While there is no universal certification board for teachers, some indications of your experience can provide a self-check. The feedback of the group should parallel the proven universal markers described at each stage of development in this book. If it does not, self-examination or a consultation with a mentor is in order. You can easily be misled by clairvoyant interpretations, intellectual expectation, and hubris, your own arrogance as to the state of development. There is indeed an experimental component to developing a working group. However, it is suggested that you consult with a mentor to avoid damaging mistakes to egos, psyches, and bodies. The taking on of unnecessary karma is a sign of not only foolishness, but also an underdeveloped ego. Become clear about your abilities and the abilities of your group before progressing to these next steps.

The standing circle up until now has been a mechanism for establishing a connection of the lowest awareness, the physical body. Remember, however, that a nonphysical link is established without physical contact in the separated palms circle. This exercise may bear repeating to firmly establish the group vocabulary and experience of the lower astral. Some talented individuals who may reach astral without any preparation may find this tedious, monotonous, and boring. However, the goal of the exercise is to develop a working group with a common vocabulary. Each contribution to the capability of the circle strengthens the individual links and makes it more than the sum of the individuals.

Chapter Six

THE ASTRAL

Just as each of these realms of consciousness overlap, the energy circle discussion in chapter 5 has already introduced the next realm of consciousness, the astral. Similarly, just as there are chapter headings to divide discussion for convenience, there are devices that separate these levels of awareness as well. The formation of energy circles provides exercises to detect and transcend each realm with its limitations and gifts.

You have been using your astral sensitivity every day without being conscious of it. Although most of us discount the ability to sense it, perhaps the person sitting next to you generates an uncomfortable feeling for you: you may sense that he or she is invasive or manipulative. When these impressions are detected, you are consciously contacting upper astral energy. This is the same dynamic behind the instant like or dislike of a person. There is an energetic interaction in the subtler astral plane that you may quickly translate into a pleasant, unpleasant, or indifferent reaction.

Astral contact could also be intuition, but with some experience, this is easily differentiated. Clairvoyance and telepathic skills are derived from the ability to separate incoming information from personal interpretation. If you remain objective, you can easily determine what a feeling means versus what personal expectation thinks it ought to mean. Opposite extremes can be registered in similar ways and, consequently, can be easily confused in subjective interpretations. For example, love and hate can be expressed in similar, easily confused patterns. A little boy pulling a girl's braids is similar to a man unbraiding a woman's hair, but these similar acts have very different meanings. It is much easier to pick up extremes in feelings than it is to pick up subtleties, and this is one reason why so many untrained psychics pick up highly charged events fairly easily, while missing subtle details.

The higher astral contains the most admired emotional qualities; charity, benevolence, and love are among the many components of its fabric of emotions. The potent fluid of the astral contains desires beyond the simple animal appetites. These desires include the inspiration to paint a picture, to create music, to promote friendship, or even to prepare and share a good meal. The higher astral qualities are abundant in good people.

From the upper astral, there is a layer that may or may not be recognized by some teachers. This layer is called the *intellect*. The intellect does not occur just because you think; it is designed for the fundamental use of solving truly difficult problems. The intellect is not designed to ruminate or to consider alternatives, it leaves that to the emotional and egoic layer. In fact, considering alternatives often paralyzes the ability to solve problems since doing so invokes the emotional layer in the process. The intellect is one of the most valued tools, but one of the most difficult to transcend. Ever since Descartes promoted the limiting boundary of "I think, therefore I am," the intellect asserts that it defines what can be known. In many cases, the intellect is the limiting factor to experiencing higher awareness. Holding on to the intellect is like using the flashlight you're holding to illuminate the hand that grasps it. Transcending the intellect doesn't mean a leap to faith, but requires understanding or intuition that there are other ways to perceive higher consciousness.

So far the realms of consciousness discussed—physical, etheric, astral, and intellectual—are all mortal. They depend on bodily existence to perceive and interact. Everything above the astral is collectively called the *causal,* or fundamental cause. After the causal, you move beyond normal human processing into the transpersonal realm. The causal levels, being independent of physical form, are accessible after death.

MOVING THE GROUP FROM LOWER TO UPPER ASTRAL

In the previous chapter, the group learned to access the astral by maintaining a flow of energy in the circle while their palms were separated. Groups vary widely when it comes to the time it takes to achieve a firm establishment in the lower astral. Depending on the group makeup, it may take anywhere from a few minutes to a few months. Any longer than a few months indicates that there is something wrong with either the teacher or the group. Assuming that all is going well and the group is still experiencing abundant chi with a pure unity, the group may be led into the higher astral.

GROUP EXERCISE 10: ENTERING THE UPPER ASTRAL

The upper astral overlaps the tangible energy field of the physical by two to three feet. Imagine it as another level on the step pyramid. By now the group should be accomplished at feeling energy in the circle and overcoming the ego boundaries of separation. In fact, the group will acclimate to this level of energy and desire to explore something new. However, if there is not cohesion in the group yet, wait until there is. The desires of a few are outweighed by the common good.

1. Ask people to form the circle by joining hands. Again, remind them to keep their knees bent and their feet separated by their shoulders' width. If there are both men and women in your circle, stagger the sexes. Ask the group members to close their eyes.

2. In order to perform this transition, you should be well practiced in your personal meditation and able to achieve clarity well beyond ego desires. The group invocation or meditation can still be used

to bring the group to clarity if necessary. By now, the simple act of forming a circle should be enough to transcend the personality level. Inform the group that, as an experiment, there is going to be a change in the circle. Ask them to adjust their position if the circle changes, but to do so quietly and smoothly.

3. Be careful to join the hands behind you to maintain the integrity of the circle as you step inside to the center.

4. Though the group will reshuffle to fill the void created by your movement, ask the members to keep their eyes closed to better sense the energetic shifts in the circle. Ask for verbal feedback.

5. Your experience in the center of the circle should be quite different as well, and you may wish to report your sensations to the group. However, keep the dialogue short, as you have other work to do. When you stand in the center of the circle, you are the origin of the circle. When electromagnetic energy moves around the circle, a vertical flow of energy is created in the circle's center. Meditate for a few minutes as you stand in the center, and align yourself until you feel the flow of energy. If you do this correctly, you will sense that the group has taken a step closer to you, though they have physically remained in the same relative position.

6. After several minutes, ask the circle participants for feedback. If the experiment was successful, the group should report that they feel they have risen above the body or the circle has grown smaller. Be conscious that some people will not have the ability to detect this subtlety. Suggest that since the circle is a continuous link, if one person experiences this, then the perception of the energy shift will eventually flow to everyone else.

7. Some people will report that they feel a pressure at the top of their heads or have a light headache. This is a signal that the group has together risen into the higher astral and is prepared for the next exercise.

Be sure to emphasize the link between the body and the upper awareness. While the higher astral is not the same as the lower, it is detected very similarly in the sensations of the physical body. The entrance into astral awareness is frequently accompanied by the sensation of rushing and of motion until you enter it more fully. Some people will report the sensations of going down a long tunnel toward a destination. This mirrors the death process as described by those who have had near-death experiences. The beginning step of dying feels as if light is receding or as if you are simply going to sleep. In actuality, the person is beginning to leave the physical shell and abandon sensory perceptions for a higher realm of consciousness that does not require a physical body. Meditation and group energy work are excellent preparations for maintaining awareness through the death process.

There are other interpretations of the experience of entering upper astral. Many people report the sensation of rising through a shaft. If students rise through this shaft while still embodied, the most likely scenario is that they will automatically be drawn back to the body. Meditation effort is required to keep the vibratory energy level elevated to stay aware of the energy that was perceived as a space over your head. With enough energy and inner self-knowledge, you are able to rise up through this tunnel to its other opening. Visualize the shape of this as a very large mushroom. You may rise up the stem of the mushroom, but if focus, concentration, or energy is not maintained, you simply sink back down. If you maintain enough focus and energy, you rise into a pleasant open area.

Intellectualization or the act of talking often provides large enough distractions to abort the flow into the larger head or dome shape of the mushroom, which is the metaphor for the expanded space above ordinary mind. When you think about being up in this space, you are no longer there. The energy and focus have dissipated. With enough clarity and energy, you may move out into the great white dome and remain there. With enough discipline, you may manage to be consciously in the dome and stem spaces while at the same time being fully aware of the physical embodiment.

GROUP EXERCISE II: SANDPILE

One exercise that a group may perform to establish its identity in the astral is called *sandpile*.[1] Sandpile is a very effective metaphor for gathering chi for meditation purposes.

1. This exercise is best done in a group meditation beyond the formal invocation of your working group.

2. Once the group has collectively reached a clear space, you can read the following to them:

Directly overhead, but just out of reach, is a gate, portal, or veil that can be opened to allow passage. To reach this gate, you must build a way to reach it. The only available material is the shifting sand on the ground level. Imagine that pockets of consciousness like grains of sand rest on the floor of this room.

Now, if you can pull with your desire and intent on these grains, they will be swept together into a pile. Imagine that we all are sweeping the sand into a pile into the middle of our circle. If the grains are piled high enough to stand on, then we'll be able to reach the opening above our heads.

However, that does not ensure that you may go through. We must wait until everyone is able to reach that opening. When we are in the right position, in the right posture, at the right time, while standing on this pile of sand the opening to the next level will pull us through.

3. When you detect the group has collectively moved through this opening, you may ring a bell or, in a soft voice, ask the members to open their eyes. Then you should solicit feedback. This exercise may take several attempts before it is successful.

The sand is a metaphor for the vitality of your inner psychic energy. If you are centered and relaxed, there may be no charge or all the sand will

---

1. This exercise was adapted, with permission, from the sandpile exercise originally developed by Ron Mangravite.

be scattered without structure. You must strive to become more awake by working with the natural body energies or performing such exercises as moving energy through the brain or finding the "sweet spot" position that allows energy to flow freely within the physical body.

PERSONAL EXERCISE: FINDING THE SWEET SPOT

Contrary to many traditions that promote separation between the physical and the spiritual realms, the wisdom school process is to integrate the two. The intent is not to leave the physical body out of these processes, but to bring the divine aspects fully into the physical. This exercise assists in finding the proper posture to allow spiritual energy to flow through the body.

1. Find a comfortable seated position with the back relatively straight. Visualize a stream of energy descending into the top of your head to flow down into your body. Notice if energy flows straight through the body or if there are puddles where it doesn't pass through easily. This exercise is generally successful when done with an accomplished teacher who generates the energy descent. If you are working alone, however, there will be no question when you actually feel the energy flow.

2. Now move to a seated position without back support. Notice if the body balances naturally. Does it cave forward? Or perhaps the muscles fatigue easily when sitting unsupported. Strive to find a position where the body balances naturally. Experiment with yours. Lean a little too far forward, and then lean a little too far back. Seek the middle position where the body feels naturally balanced with the head centered on top of the spine.

3. With a little experimentation, or if you have been evolving a good meditation posture, you may find a place where the body sits without tension and energy flows more noticeably.

4. When you find this position, the flow of energy through your body increases. It is oh so sweet. When you find this "sweet spot,"

the body rocks gently back and forth in balance with your breathing. You may find it difficult to leave this blissful, sweet place.

The sweet spot is an effective method for individuals to gain access to
more energy while performing the sandpile exercise. In a group, if the
chi or sand is too low and spread apart, then the group is instructed to
find more energy to focus and create the rise in the center. The sweet
spot is just one available resource. Another possibility is to remember
levels of awareness previously attained in standing circles. The group
memory often stimulates that same level and brings energy into the
low areas. Additionally, an advanced teacher may bring in a charge of
energy by spanning multiple levels and allowing that energy to discharge into the group. A small bit of higher consciousness expands
exponentially when brought down into a lower level of awareness.
This injection of chi into a group can almost immediately lead the
group straight up, or the additional energy may cause the mind to
want to be active someplace else. If the energy is not carefully monitored and shaped, then the sandpile is trampled and becomes inca-
pable of supporting the group. Therefore, you are walking a fine line
between total relaxation, where the sand spreads out and the group
mind begins to drift unfocused, and the opposite extreme of a highly
charged state that the group is unable to sustain. Beginning groups
may have to be led several times through this exercise, but when members achieve its reward, it is never forgotten. Once they feel the open
expansive awareness, the group no longer requires this kind of exercise. A simple reminder of its title almost guarantees a unified combination resulting in a higher energy level.

Many people report that the upper astral resembles a great dome-
shaped realm at the top of a perceived traveled shaft. By looking down
the end of it, it appears as a cone where there seems to be a bubble of
blue. This blue light, when localized in your head, is called the *blue
pearl.* This yogic technique is a specialization of concentrating everything to a controllable point. This is in exact opposition to the Zen
tradition that defocuses everything while maintaining awareness.

Indeed, to find the middle path as suggested by Buddhism, many groups will blend both styles of meditation.

GROUP EXERCISE 12: DETECTING THE GROUP IDENTITY IN THE ASTRAL

Explore the group connection in meditation by using visualization.

1. Have the group meditate together. This doesn't have to be done in a circle.

2. Ask the members to keep their eyes closed and to rely on their inner senses for the next step.

3. Invite the individuals to sense the boundaries of their bodies from the inside. Suggest that they move their awareness to various areas—the throat, heart, legs, feet, heel, little finger, and so on.

4. Ask the group to sense the boundary of the skin. Notice how the skin is the interface or membrane between what is inside of them and what is outside. Be aware of the air that touches the skin.

5. Suggest a focus on the breath, since breath brings the outside into the body. Notice that the air is transformed by this process—the composition and temperature is changed. Let your awareness become the air that moves in and out of your body.

6. Notice that when you are identifying with the air, you are sharing the same atmosphere with the other group members. Notice how the air particles intermingle and exchange without discrimination. Breathe deeply.

7. Now, in the mind's eye, let yourself feel the experience of the breath as it moves in and out of the group. Sense how it feels to be in the other bodies. Visualize the other group members while keeping your eyes closed.

8. Stay in silence for several moments while breathing deeply.

ISSUES OF ENTERING THE ASTRAL

The extension out of the body is simply a question of dealing with fear. You must leave a realm that is defined primarily by your physical senses. This abandonment of your personal universe may be cause for some anxiety. For many, it may feel like standing at the edge of the trapeze platform. You must risk leaving the safety of the solidity of its base and jumping off into space with the hope of swinging out on the trapeze bar. This abandonment of the known for the unknown is terrifying for some people, and will arise often at different stages of development.

Another component inhibiting the rise into upper astral is the ability to sense without intellectualizing. This realm should not be so easily defined as being either body or not body. The brain certainly belongs to the physical body, but the mind encompasses more than the organ that houses it. The combination of mind and brain developed the tool of intellect, a useful device for analysis and problem solving, but a contraindication of the full awareness of astral. In the upper astral, you can be conscious, but not thinking.

The concept of emotional judgment returns in the upper astral realms. Many students express concerns regarding safety. This indication of lack of unity is important. If a student feels safe with another being, feels cared about, then the separate energies flow together and generally achieve a higher awareness collectively. This merger often reflects what most psychically sensitive people feel automatically as the benefits of love and relationship. The connections generated by the student/teacher, doctor/client, healer/patient create a conscious space created by their relationship.

The upper astral presents almost a lifetime of work since most students will find their identity there. Students become open to the collective unconscious that is a repository of an incredible amount of information. At the upper astral level, this information is not limited by time. Some individuals may encounter knowledge of their past actions, generally referred to as *karma*. The records of these actions reflect only the deed performed by the fundamental energy, or *essence,* rather than the relatively low level of personality. For this reason many people do not obtain minute details of their past, but general themes.

Once the group begins to function in the higher astral, not only do individual tensions and illusions emerge, but also those of the collective unconscious. Frequently the dream life begins to reveal all the stress within an individual. Some refer to these dreams as *processing dreams* since these Freudian or Jungian interpreted dreams cause internal churning and discomfort until the ego resolves the tension. The tensions encountered generally appear as threats to the psyche. The discomfort arises because threats are perceived far more readily than benevolence. Indeed, ego and the reptilian developed portion of your brain, the hindbrain, are designed to look for such threats to ensure our survival. Most telepathic and clairvoyant messages are warnings about something that may be a threat because it takes far more awareness to override the body's prioritization for its survival purposes. The gateways of perception are not opened as easily for beneficial occurrences.

Much personal clearing and ego work can be done with the awareness of the dream state of the upper astral. Dreams bring up any threats—usually emotional threats, and, occasionally, physical ones. Your problems from the past may all surface—the personal slights, inferiority complexes, abandonment issues, and so on. At death, the abandonment of sensory perception allows this same vulnerability to arise. Any concern that makes you vulnerable will emerge. One key to remember: no one is vulnerable except through fear. Nothing can be done to anyone. The body can be caused to feel pain. An unhealthy ego can be made to feel emotional pain. Other than that, your being is invulnerable to anyone else. Unfortunately, the body and lower self frequently control our ordinary awareness and forget its invulnerability. Therefore, in the dream state arises deep memories, neuroses, and psychoses that must be resolved. Your vulnerabilities continue to manifest until the nature of the fear on which they are based is identified.

The most effective way to remember invulnerability is to "die" to our fears. The power fear has over us disappears when it has already exerted the maximum affect on us. In corporate sales training, you are taught to imagine that the worst possible outcome occurs. In planning for that event, you frequently find the invulnerable warrior aspect emerging. For many people, their greatest fear is death. Indeed, that is why so many initiatory experiences invoke a near-death experience that stimulates invulnerability. As far as the subconscious is concerned, "If I let this happen, I will die." If you are willing to let it happen and experience psychological death, it can't hurt anymore. This is far easier to say than to do.

CONTRAINDICATIONS

The process of dismantling your psyche requires an immovable center or a true identity. With a true self, no one else can affect that center without your consent. The practice of meditation develops an energy center. If you cannot develop a true identity, then transformative meditation should not be practiced, as it is a serious attempt at restructuring your entire self. If there is not some kind of healthy structure to begin with, instead of disassembling self, there is a regression into infantile states. A substantial number of the population should not undertake serious meditation. Certainly a young child should not meditate, but can be encouraged to identify his or her body sensation through the development of an ego. With an ego, the child develops boundaries and learns to live in society. The civilization of an unrestrained child into a civilized human is necessary, but it may also destroy the natural capacity of a total telepathic and mystical link. You can encourage a child to stay open to the passage of his or her emotional and spiritual flow while developing the social skills and manners necessary for the culture.

It would be nice to think that once the psychological death is accomplished, the work of astral is complete. It isn't. Having processed your own issues or "junk," you are now faced with the issues of the collective unconscious as they manifest in the astral. You may find universal stress and tension. Patterns of fundamental myths of the higher patterns or archetypal layer may emerge in astral work. In the subconscious, you may find psychological enactments of the myths of Atlantis, Lemuria, and so on, or themes such as the creator and destroyer. Ultimately, you must have enough identity to separate self from myth.

TRUE IDENTITY and PSYCHOLOGICAL DISORDERS

True identity can recognize itself while doing activities without the activities changing it. The finding of your true identity is the key for transformation. When a person can shift the individual vibration to some higher elevated space and be totally aware of the process without inhibiting it, true identity is found.

True identity begins to emerge at various levels in degraded form, even in the case of simple hypocrisy, such as, "How are you? You look great," while thinking, "Am I talking too loud? Did they really give me a funny look?" This level of mental activity, while symptomatic of a neurotic personality, is also an indication of a larger true identity's operation. The neurosis is masking a higher awareness that observes the environment in great detail. Some neurotic group members do not respond to meditation work, and some of their inherent difficulties may not be revealed until after they join the group. There is a risk in keeping such members, but their true identities may eventually emerge and contribute greatly to the group. Therefore, group candidates with neurotic tendencies should be examined carefully before dismissing them from the group. You should be aware that over time, group members come and go, but as the balance of energies is maintained, the group continues.

Another psychological disorder, schizophrenia, has another perspective when true identity is taken in consideration. There may or may not be a higher identity functioning in another level of awareness, causing dysfunction of awareness of actions and process in consensual reality. Your true identity may demand total absorption to function at a higher level. An accomplished teacher may meditate with such a person and examine both the subtle maneuvers and the consciousness that belongs to the higher level. A being is totally absorbed at its natural upper level.

THE DETECTION OF MEMBRANES IN GROUP CIRCLES

The concept of membranes that divide levels of awareness should be addressed since the major obstacle of a group is to penetrate these dividers of realms. In a standing energy circle, the barrier of the astral can be easily demonstrated. The teacher, having formed or sensed unity in the group, lifts the group to the upper limit of the astral, as explained in former exercises.

In your next group meeting, you will require the members to feel the body's weight, as fundamental grounding is necessary for the individuals. It only takes one person hitting the floor facedown to remember to establish a ground before bringing in higher energies. With a solid group ground connection, the group members sense each individual without losing the unified sense of group. When the group energy is achieved and detected, the space opens above the group with the merging of the energies. By routinely starting at the lower astral level and gradually opening to the higher levels, it is very hard to make a misstep.

As the group rises to the upper limit of the astral, some participants feel a rising sensation and others report that it feels as if the tops of their heads are hitting a ceiling of some type. This is an indication that you are beginning to feel the physical sensations of coming up against the astral barrier. The barrier is felt only if you are directly in the central shaft of the level of awareness. In the center, the emphasis is on transforming the vibration to a higher plane as opposed to just progressing to the next level. The attempt to move through this barrier generates the group to apply more energy, but still nothing is happening. Like a revving engine that is not in gear, the motor is racing but nothing is engaged and no one is moving. This is the first barrier or membrane encountered on a progressive meditation map. It requires a guru or a change in being to cross the membrane.

The leader meditates to the clearest space of his or her true identity while being quite aware of the grounding force established earlier. By holding awareness at two different levels, energy flows between the members. While the leader may experience the flow of energy, the group may feel a sudden release of the pressure of the membrane. While the group members may feel the result, they may or may not feel the exact mechanism, which is similar to moving through a backward question mark–shaped passageway. This very important and very subtle transition frequently takes more than one exposure to detect.

GROUP EXERCISE 13: MEMBRANE DETECTION

This exercise is best done in an established standing circle, one that has worked together for several sessions.

1. The leader asks the members to become aware of their physical bodies and allows time to adjust to feeling just the energy that fills their bodies. As this is done, the attention is shifted to feel the group's energy and identity.

2. Now you may find the highest, clearest space you know, and share that with the circle. Imagine that you are a sphere of white light. With each breath you make that sphere larger until it reaches the individual spheres of group members. Projecting true identity into the group is accomplished when the teacher lets the group be an extension of his or her own being and psyche. Remind the group verbally that every participant owns the circle. You cannot be lost in a circle; you can only gain it.

3. The teacher lifts the awareness of the group to the upper limit of the astral by bridging higher awareness to the ground of the group and allowing energy to flow into the circle. The clarity of the individual flows into the sphere of light and is shared with every being within its reach.

4. Ask the members of the group if they noticed a change. While the act of asking for a response suggests to participants that there is a change, which may influence them, in actuality, this is a desired conditioning. General feedback of pressure in the head, headaches, or even anxiety and frustration are some common signs of sensing the barrier.

5. The group is now prepared to go through the barrier. As you lead the members into the causal realm, some may report that a hole or chamber seems to have opened over their head. Others may report that the top of the head may open and feel expanded.

6. Hold the group at this level until all members sense a change of quality in the space. Searching for descriptions by the participants is discouraged. This barrier can only be detected through experience. The subtlety of going through this barrier often prevents people from attaining higher levels of meditation, as they have not the vaguest idea of what just happened.

7. When the barrier is penetrated, your shared comments build metaphors and similes that assist in recognizing the process. While the group identity gives you the ability to achieve higher awareness than the astral, everyone must eventually learn to do this individually and integrate the process.

You may not experience anything the first time you attempt this. Many people cannot hold consciousness and simply blank out during the process. Anyone who felt some form of change going through the astral barrier was probably there. For those individuals, they must simply achieve familiarity with the passageway. The passage through the barrier is accompanied by a release of pressure or containment. A useful metaphor is walking hunched over through the confined space leading to the King's Chamber in the Great Pyramid. After the minutes of half-crawling through tight quarters, the welcome space to stand up and move unencumbered is liberating.

Others sense the astral as being an extension of their physical body. They describe it as feeling lighter or as growing taller. Their body seems to extend into a realm two to three feet above their head as the senses of one realm extend into another. Like the wedding cake or step pyramid analogy, the second layer is built upon the larger layer below it. The astral is, in actuality, always surrounding and interpenetrating, but as a group is learning, the step pyramid gives them scaffolding for their understanding.

There are several purposes for being able to detect the astral barrier. First, when you are working individually, the focus may dissipate, in which case you slide back down the shaft. If this happens, you cannot only recognize it, but you can build energy to rise up and rejoin the group. Second, you eventually face this same barrier shortly before or after the death of the physical body. This energy circle practice allows you to experience awareness without being dependent on the physical body. Eventually you will find this useful for maintaining consciousness during the death process. While still in physical form, though, much work may be done without having gone through that barrier. If you are able to achieve it, the knowledge of all human purpose, endeavor, and condition will become available. In many ways, you have effectively died before you have physically died.

The *astral,* meaning "of the stars," is a stage of meditation that opens a new world to discover. You can spend an entire lifetime exploring the astral. Many societies and magical organizations, for example, expend a great deal of energy entering and working in these realms. For many who recognize or have been shown a higher level of operating, such groups may provide a useful introduction to astral work. For others, they are a means to becoming lost in exploring fantasies or trying to control others and the world from this low realm.

The astral is easily accessible; you have this experience nightly when you sleep and dream. The astral body, sometimes referred to as the dream body, is not subject to the limitations of the physical body. You may fly in dreams, instantly travel thousands of miles, and meet people you haven't thought of in years. When you are in a vivid dream, you frequently assume that it is real. In the astral there can be many illusionary sensory experiences as well as interchanges with other astral entities. The astral is a normal awareness in the dream state that most of us choose to forget in everyday interactions.

Some students report that an artificial method of entering the astral in the waking state is through the smoking of marijuana, though I personally don't recommend the ingestion of any drug. They report an easy entrance allowing the experience of heightened senses where colors are brighter, food tastes better, and perception is sensitized. In many ways, marijuana brings the heightened senses of the dream world into everyday awareness. Drug use, particularly hallucinogens, has been part of many initiations. The Mayan-Aztec culture figured the use prominently. In the Greek mysteries of Eleusis, ergot of barley was their agent of choice. Soma, a mushroom product, was disclosed as part of the Vedic sacraments. In the last century, Aldous Huxley's recordings of his experiences with mescaline, and Timothy Leary's and Ram Dass' explorations of LSD led into mystical and altered awareness. However, there is no reason to use drugs. You have the ability to train yourself to live in the astral and physical planes simultaneously. Meditation and yogic dream work are more permanent and less toxic ways to enter and explore the astral realm. At your moment of death, you will automatically enter the astral plane. Meditation teaches you how to interact at that level as well as how to move on to higher consciousness. Later, you may find that it is more effective to enter the astral from the level above instead of struggling to build energy from below. As higher energy is brought into a lower level, an enormous amount of vitality is released and the group is immediately brought to a high peak of awareness.

The astral is built from the realm of feeling—not personal emotion, but feeling without egoic constraints. Any energy without personal involvement may be used to consciously enter the astral. Many magical societies use blood sacrifices, shared sexuality, or stimulating energetic rituals to accomplish their entry into the astral realm. Regardless of the method of entry into the astral, you are initially introduced to a nonphysical reality, enhanced perception, dreams, and flying.

Yet, the astral serves far more esoteric purposes than mere "fun trips" in alternate spaces. Many mystery schools and esoteric traditions preserve one of the original purposes of astral interactions. The Qabalistic Tree of Life (see figure 4, page 132) places the sephirah for the astral realm just above the mundane one. This realm serves as a blueprint for creating the physical world, and is the reason why spells and magic so often work. Ritual magic may use the resources of the physical world to enter the astral. In the astral, the blueprints for the physical manifestation of objects and events can be manipulated. These altered blueprints, in turn, affect the manifestation and interactions of objects in the mundane world.

In meditation or actual astral travel, there is an easily recognized, dull, soft glow that brightens as the astral interactions become more involved. This differentiation of color provides an easy division of the astral into sublayers, known as *lower astral* and *higher astral*. The lower levels are perceived as a luminous fog that changes color. If an individual is more intellectually inclined, the fog appears golden; likewise, the fog will appear blue if the individual is more sensory oriented. In the upper astral, the lighting takes on a bluish or ultraviolet quality that makes colors appear more vivid and vibrant. In earlier times, most of humanity was unable to perceive the color blue. Consequently, the sea was described by some as being "wine-dark." Only those on the level of the gods or royalty were able to perceive blue or purple, indicating a higher perceptual ability to the bluebloods. The mysteries of the pyramid and tomb murals were written in blue to ensure their secrecy.

The lower astral encompasses powerful, nonintellectual body needs and desires such as hunger, sex, and fear. These are basic first chakra needs—ensuring the survival of the body. The lower astral permeates the physical realm. As a distinction from conventional solid matter, the astral can be considered a fluid. Water is a fluid, air is a fluid, and

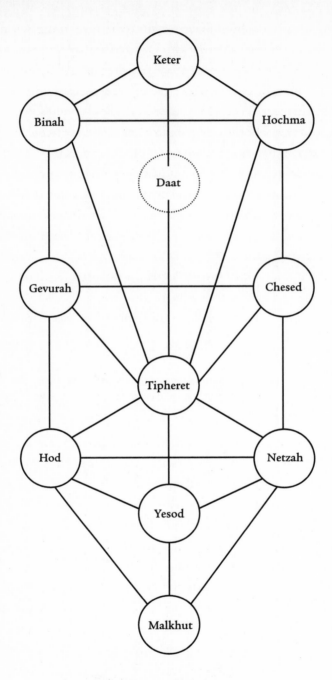

Figure 4: The Tree of Life.

the astral is a fluid. The human body is comprised mainly of water, the fluid of the physical realm, and provides the substance for manifestation. Everywhere a physical body exists, there is a pattern that causes an interruption or an anomaly in the flow of the fluid. The pattern that holds the fluid together in the physical is found in the astral realm. This blueprint is made of astral fluid, and its affect is converted through the etheric realm to create physical forms.

The astral is both useful and seductive in its vast powers to imagine, to heal, and to dream. Yet, for the initiate, there is more to discover on the spiritual path.

WHITE WOLf: AN ASTRAL VISITATION

There is such freedom in flying—no set paths and few restrictions. I was flying through the air in my dream. Soaring through the night sky, I was headed home. Just as I was about to reenter my sleeping body, I realized there were strange beings encircling it. I stopped short, observing this strange and confusing situation. The beings, tall and made of translucent light, arranged my body in a particular position, almost as if I were a doll. They folded my hands across my body and flexed one leg under the other in the same bent-leg position as the Hanged Man in the tarot deck.

Alarmed, I hurriedly reentered my body and awoke in the physical world to hear rustling noises in my bedroom. Immobilized from fear or some other reason, I couldn't even open my eyes! Yet I realized that my physical body was in exactly the same position I had seen in my "dream." There was substantial movement around me. Using all my will power, I attempted to gain control over my body. Failing, I decided to concentrate my efforts to move one finger.

"SHH! She's awake."

My efforts alerted them that I was aware of them. Had they really spoken or had I heard them telepathically? If only I could see them, I might be able to make sense of these events. I struggled to move my finger. All of their activities immediately ceased. Then a moderate vibration shook the floor and my bed. Without reasoning ability, I concluded that their ship, hovering over my pasture, was causing this phenomenon.

The rustling noises began again, and I could sense these light beings moving in the room. I renewed my effort to move. Movement might break the paralysis. I concentrated on my right hand index finger. "Move," I urged it. "Stretch. Move." I felt no connection to my body. I was concentrating more than I ever had on anything, yet I was still unable to move my finger. The rustling was gone now, and the vibration diminished, but I discovered a weight on my leg.

Stacy must have let my dog in and Sugar's jumped up on the bed, I thought. Then I remembered that not only had Stacy moved out three weeks ago, she had also taken Sugar with her.

Now, I had to move my finger. I redoubled my efforts and finally flexed the tip of the index finger through dogged concentration. Many seconds later I extended my finger, and reached out to touch the animal on the bed. As I touched his coat, I inexplicably was able to open my eyes. There, asleep on my legs and facing the bed's footboard, was what appeared to be a large, long-haired, white dog. He stirred as I touched him, and turned his face to me. He was a white wolf! His eyes had white light for irises that radiated pure hypnotizing love to me. My whole being was fascinated, and I forgot about the light visitors, who left without my noticing them. Suddenly, I sensed a vibration of a "ship" leaving and received the instruction, "Go to sleep." So I did.

In the morning, everything seemed normal. No wolf anywhere. However, I didn't forget the experience. In fact, I began tracking down every clue that I could to understand why a white wolf would have appeared to me. Many days later, I noticed a small ad in the local paper announcing that the Quest Society was sponsoring a talk by Morgan Medicine Bear that evening. If I hurried, I had just enough time to make the seminar.

The Quest Society met in an old, run-down motel that rented one of its dining rooms for meetings. Approximately fifty people had gathered to hear the Native American speak passionately about the land, his heritage, and current events. His speech ran over the allotted time and there was no time for questions. I was disappointed. Something about this man gave me the sense he could help me, so I followed him out to the parking lot, where he had gone to have a cigarette. I waited impatiently, as someone else was already talking to him.

"Now I have to go," he stated and headed for his car.

Summoning courage to overcome my shyness, I couldn't let this opportunity slip by. Having already reached his car, I ran to it and tapped on his closed car window.

"Please, I need your help and I don't know where else to turn," I pleaded.

The old man looked at me and rolled down the window.

"Yes."

"I had a white wolf come visit me and I don't know what it means." I gave him the short version of the story. When I finished, he took a deep breath and carefully considered me.

"The place you will find the answer is a sacred Cherokee place where the quartz rock stands as guardian of the merger of three flowing waters." He started to roll up the car window as he finished speaking.

"Wait, please. There are thousands of acres in the Cherokee reservations here. Can't you please help me narrow it down?"

"Near here," was his only reply as he rolled up his window, put his old rusty brown Pontiac in reverse, and sped away.

I was devastated. To make a long story short, I spent the next few weekends driving through the reservation areas within range of my home. Months later, I was no closer and the passion to know began to subside. However, years later, returning from a buying trip in the mountains, I stopped at a roadside park where I had heard there was a delightful picnic area. The drive in was rugged, but soon opened into an empty paved parking area. I pulled into the first parking space.

This small park was below highway level, giving it a seclusion that belied its location, which was so close to a well-traveled road. I looked around me, not knowing quite what to expect here. Then I realized that immediately in front of my trusty Honda was a huge quartz boulder standing like a lighthouse guarding the wooded trails to the picnic area. Later I learned that the stone belonged to a wise Cherokee woman who encoded her wisdom within it when she was forced to leave it behind in her sacred land during the Trail of Tears. The presence of the quartz rock was intriguing and reminded me of the white wolf incident months earlier.

I noticed a wooded path leading into a picnic area and began to walk. With each step, I seemed to be leaving the world of cars, stores, and people farther behind. As I crested a small hill, I noted that there were two streams merging under the rustic log bridge. Crossing over, I stepped off the main path into a fern glade. There, hidden beneath the green fronds, I noted that there was an additional influence to the stream. There were actually three streams merging together at this point. All the hair on my body stood up as energy rushed through me and I realized that I had found the elusive land I had sought for so long. I was there.

Though I knew my car was the only one in the parking lot, I could now hear the youthful bantering voices on the cliff above me. Allowing my inner senses to take in the scene, I realized that this was an initiation site for Native Americans—sacred to women. The elder women were leading the girls to the hidden waterfall, where the ritual would mark their transition into young women. I knew them, and I knew this site. Forever, I would be bringing women here to remind them of the sacredness of the land, our role in society, and our wisdom.

Chapter Seven

THE CAUSAL THRESHOLD
INTO THE ARCHETYPAL

While all of humanity inherently has access to the etheric, physical, and astral levels, the causal levels frequently require the assistance of a guru or teacher. Most people require additional energy beyond their own and are given threshold energy through darshan, a transmission of higher energies by a teacher. Another useful technique is to combine the energy from the circle you built earlier. The shared identity within a working circle allows a balance of individual strengths and weaknesses to form a higher entity with more energy. The shared circle provides energy to carry you beyond your personal limitations until you develop enough tools to access the causal directly. Regardless of the energy source, as you penetrate the barrier into the causal realm, you have also crossed another significant boundary. The causal realm is not dependent on the energies of the physical body; if you are able to stay conscious there, you have technically met the requirement for immortality. Some Buddhist traditions refer to this immortal existence as the diamond, or permanent body.

Survival of consciousness without the use of a physical body requires that a human being be willing to transcend the human ego and body limitations. Additionally, you must learn to maintain enough chi to maintain consciousness. The entrance into the causal often is a test of your own preparation. The physical body issues you've addressed may yield successfully to your meditation, but the emotional aspects may go haywire. You may then resolve the psychological issues only to have the physical body resist in a new way. The untangling of your body issues and psyche trauma or karma may seem to be an endurance test at times. However, the transcendence of your human construct is necessary to penetrate the causal levels.

The average ego considers the transformative process a threat to existence. The closer you approach the causal, the more the body, emotions, and motivations will scream to stop this painful process. Doubts of self, process, and teacher frequently are prevalent. One or many of these confrontational aspects must be encountered before you actually may transcend into the causal. When you do find access to the causal, it is a feeling of having been reborn.

The good news is that once you have made it into the causal, most of the glitches in the body and psyche are well-known. This is extremely helpful in that if you slip back into the ego and physical issues it is far easier to regain access to the higher realm a second time. Few people, if any, ever achieve constant awareness of the archetypal level permanently. However, even a one-time experience transforms you completely. You live your everyday life without being influenced by unknown ego aspects. You act with more clarity, mindfulness, and wisdom. You also possess the meditative tools to regain the archetypal awareness when needed. The psycho-spiritual work of untangling emotional and body issues that facilitated entrance into the archetypal layer continues to reveal suppressed material. Your entire history, recorded in your ancient DNA and timeless mind, continues to bring patterns of your life to awareness. In the causal, however, instead of being trapped by the process, you are exalted by it.

THE ARCHETYPAL SELF

As your transpersonal identity is found, you may explore the various substratums of energetic vibrations. Normally, you may find the archetypal realm, where existence is not as a single individual but is the embodiment of a single specialized quality of consciousness.

Archetypes can be distinguished by such qualities as compassion, benevolence, warrior, and teacher aspects. Though others may categorize archetypes within their own systems, you may find it more valuable to feel these energies on your own terms. Then, according to your structure, you may assign labels or names to them. While the average person is comprised of several archetypal principles, there are a few individuals who embrace a pure quality fully. These enlightened beings are known as *avatars*. You may consider the late Mother Teresa an example of a modern-day avatar.

You, on the other hand, may have to explore several archetypal qualities that you have hidden in your super-conscious. By successfully practicing the energy circles defined in chapter 6, you may uncover surprising information. Whether individually or collectively in meditation, the astral reveals clues to the archetypal energies. You find the natural energy that contains the Atlantean myth, or the watery realms of Lemuria. On a more practical note, you may find complete dramas that reflect directly into the dynamics of your everyday life. For example, in meditation I connected with Artemis, the virgin goddess. On another occasion, I found an image of the Arthurian Guinevere. These two images reflect similar qualities for me. Personally, these images were a higher reflection concerning the gifts and sufferings associated with the inability to conceive children. Each archetypal energy presents a perspective that assists in resolving the issue of barrenness. No wonder certain cultures still call on the archetypal images to shape events in their lives.

Also, do not be overly distressed if you encounter weird phenomena during meditation or ritual within the archetypal realm. The point is to be detached; neither block it out nor act upon it. Many of these psychic events are a discharge of toxins. If you do not identify with them, you facilitate a healthy process for the toxins to be emerging, processed, and digested.

The healthy human being, when transiting from the astral to the archetypal, may find rapid movement through the dark tunnel from the astral barrier. Suddenly, there is an explosion into a totally different awareness that is archetypal. If you are not ready for it, there is either nothing there or fear will make you turn back. The usually helpful analytic aspect of intellect may detect this space as empty and revert back to some awareness it can detect—the physical body. In other words, your fear immediately returns your concerns to physical matters. Be gentle with yourself. This work of initiation is challenging. The new landscape is just another degree of subtlety.

While the achievement of the archetypal is important for you, the group is also integrating this stage. The energy circles, which frequently cause dramatic experiences and reactions, are reintroduced into more subtle applications in the transformative meditation system. Instead of each individual meditating privately, the same methods used physically to establish a working group are now applied through the astral into the archetypal. There is a blending of the group members into their archetypal families to form a combined unified identity. If your group is able to work without any of the ego projections, chanting provides a simple, but proven, method to establish an archetypal identity in meditation. Begin the following exercise with a relaxed, established group.

GROUP EXERCISE 14: CHANTING TO CREATE A HIGHER IDENTITY

Begin with some centered breathing as the established circle has done before.

1. Take a deep breath and allow your body to relax as you exhale. Adjust your posture so that you may feel your chest expand and contract. Breathe deeply and allow your belly to be relaxed and full. Some people are chest breathers while others breathe from the belly. Use your full diaphragm to its greatest capacity.

2. As you find your own rhythm of deep breathing, we're going to add another dimension to this exercise by using a particular pat-

tern of breathing. With your next breath, breathe in through your nose, but exhale through your mouth. Let your focus establish this pattern without thinking.

3. This time, when you exhale, let your voice make an audible, full, long "O" sound. Pick a tone that feels comfortable for you, and don't be afraid to experiment with each exhalation.

4. Keep doing this until you are doing it automatically, without thinking or worrying about it. Let yourself be lost in the rhythm.

5. We'll keep doing this until something very special and unplanned occurs. The exercise ends when there is a spontaneous blend in the individual tones to a group harmony. The group notes their achievement, and with practice can move immediately from chanting into a silent, shared meditation.

The meditation is not about individuals meditating in the same location at the same time; it is now a meditation where a singular identity comprised of group members meditates. At this significant accomplishment, the teacher whose identity has always been a part of the group may add and shift energies to create and shape other levels of experiences.

GROUP EXERCISE 15: CONSCIOUS ACTS IN UNISON

Performing acts consciously together creates enormous energy, clarity, and focus. Frequently, thoughts, emotions, and personality drop away as a group chants. (I learned the chant used in this exercise at a retreat in a Monday evening Kirtan, an Indian celebration of god/spirit. When I sing this one, I feel that unified expression of love that was shared there and evoke connections I know from my experiences. The verse is sung repeatedly in unison, building to a crescendo and then fading away to its normal conclusion organically; by doing this you let the energy rise through you, carry you to new heights, and return to the body. It's all about bringing the divine love into full expression within you.)

1. Encourage everyone to sing, regardless of whether they can carry a tune or not. Just as a circle requires everyone to participate to form a group identity, so does singing.

2. Most likely, no one in the group will know the correct pronunciation of these words. Remind the group that as children they learned by joining in and imitating. Suspend judgment. Have childlike fun with this.

3. Since no music is included here, if no one knows the chant you may either purchase a tape that includes it or make up your own tune. For more fun, have someone different make up a tune for each line.

   Gopala, gopala, devikanandana gopala.
   (Gō pă lă, gō pă lă, dā věk a năn dănă, gō pă lă.)

   Gopala, gopala, devikanandana gopala.
   (Gō pă lă, gō pă lă, dā věk a năn dănă, gō pă lă.)

   Devikanandana gopala, devikanadana gopala.
   (Dā věk a năn dănă, gō pă lă, dā věk a năn dănă, gō pă lă.)

   Devikanandana gopala, devikanadana gopala.
   (Dā věk a năn dănă, gō pă lă, dā věk a năn dănă, gō pă lă.)

4. Ask someone in the group to obtain a recording of this chant so that you can compare your results. Explore how the different renditions affect the group's state of consciousness. Sanskrit, a language used to describe sacred events, uses the sounds and the words to convey higher meaning.

The leader of Kirtan taught us that Sanskrit is more about the sounds and spirit than the intellectual translation. He said that most chants could be loosely translated as "Praise God." Indeed, Sanskrit is an elite language where the sounds, artistry of letters, and expression are perhaps more sacred than the thought forms expressed in words. Use blended voices through song or chant to easily build a group identity that may access the archetypal realm.

THE ARCHETYPAL LAYER

Through the energy circle experiences and through the creation of a meditation identity, you emerge as a well-prepared initiate into the transpersonal level. A teacher's guidance is very valuable in the causal because when you are fully functional in the casual, whatever you will usually happens. *Will* is defined here as "a spiritually inspired act of volition." While the group identity may be extremely clear of ego projections and desires, it is still possible for the individual to be caught up in games of power and attention.

Note, however, that you cannot individually will until you personally have risen above the previous ego levels by integrating their energies, resolving issues, and becoming functional in combining energies in them. The lack of egoic desire is possibly the reason that powerful mystics do not manipulate their gifts to obtain winning lottery numbers or the like.

You should also be aware that many students mistake the premonitions or forerunners of all the causal states for the real event. Since the group identity has achieved it, a member may project that he or she has achieved it alone. Personal illusions can be difficult to release, and you must be alert for these common traps for the spiritual initiate. Adding to the difficulty of distinguishing personal versus group ability is that for some period you may actually know these higher realms. However, the memory is eventually lost because you have not been in those states long enough to read and accept the territory. Integration is a slow process that gains momentum. The first step may take you twenty minutes, a year, twenty years, or a lifetime. The second step takes half the time; the next step requires half the time again. Like any real process, frustrating discipline and a dogged commitment eventually produce a truly functional being. Perhaps because of the previous work of other groups, this time interval generally is growing much shorter. Enlightenment in a lifetime is far easier now than at any other point in history.

The passage through the natural division, or membrane, dividing the archetypal layer from the astral is the single most valuable experience to an initiate. This knowledge, before death or at death, allows you to leave the mortal realm and enter into the realm of the immortals. In my understanding of the Christian teachings, this is one of the major mysteries of the crucifixion of Jesus. Having been a great initiate, Jesus was able to penetrate the membrane of the astral before his physical death. In effect, he was able to achieve a level of consciousness that until that moment in time was only achievable at death. He effectively died before he physically died. Though his disciples and a few others presumably achieved this same ability, the masses could not understand the higher layers of consciousness. Only when Paul spread the news of Jesus' physical death and his appearance afterward did this information become available in mass consciousness. Jesus' death and acknowledged resurrection gave humanity the blueprint to find life everlasting. The archetypal blueprint as well as a pure archetypal expression of Jesus the Christ remain today.

The archetypal layer is also inhabited by primal, unembodied forces, called *devas*. The devic presences form Rupert Sheldrake's concept of morphogenic fields.[1] Sheldrake states that matter arranges itself according to the blueprint within it. Additionally, you may consider that the field continues to acquire experience and wisdom. Each expression of the species adds to the generic morphogenic field. The pattern then contains the culmination of experiences of the species. Similarly, when you enter the realm of the archetypes, you contribute your experiences and results into the realm of the collective spiritual blueprint. Your experiences contribute to the pattern that shapes all of humanity.

---

1. Rupert Sheldrake, *A New Science of Life: The Hypothesis of Morphic Resonance* (Rochester, Vt.: Park Street Press, 1995), 12–13.

fINDINg MYTHIC ROLES

When conscious in the archetypal realm, you enter a library of all human experiences through myths and stories representing common archetypal themes. For example, the tale of King Arthur, Guinevere, and Lancelot may provide insight into resolving the problems of unrequited love, a loveless marriage, and a partner's or friend's betrayal. The love triangle myth earned its popularity because so many people identity with their dilemmas. Each character in the story provides a unique perspective to the situation. By enacting the myth or watching a dramatic play unfold, you gain multiple perspectives on an event.

Other stories, such as *Alice in Wonderland* or *The Wizard of Oz,* serve as parables in dealing with adventures into new territories. New feature films and stories provide arising themes in current society that also provide useful tools for psychological self-examination. If you are involved in a situation that seems unresolvable, try to find a myth or plot that is close to your situation. Assign the players in your situation to the names of the mythic characters and see how they interact. If you can find an appropriate myth, then you may understand the interactions of yourself and others more clearly. To gain additional insight, you may attempt to identify with all the mythic roles. Frequently, I find that I must successfully play all the roles in the myth before I break free of the archetypal pattern.

Finding a mythic role can be used to gain perspective on daily activities as well. Be careful not to confuse mythic roles with personal past lives. Generally, you can distinguish the archetypal by noting that there is nothing personal there. The mythic roles may indeed be a part of your karmic family, but usually you are facing dynamics emerging from the lower emotional realm. Remember, not everyone was Cleopatra, yet everyone may be a part of her archetypal story. You may remember the stories, but do not invest your time and energy into claims of personal association. Eventually, if you achieve a functional mystical identity, you may use the concept of parallel lives. All existences are separated by space and time. For now, the focus should remain on understanding the archetypal principles on your spiritual quest.

INDIVIDUAL Or GROUP EXERCISE: FINDING A MYTHIC ROLE

1. Have a pencil and paper for this exercise. Be comfortable and relaxed, and give yourself at least thirty minutes for this session.

2. Take a few deep breaths to become centered and focused.

3. Let your favorite book, story, or legend come to mind.

4. List the following:

   • Setting

   • Description of main character

   • Description of antagonist

   • Nature of the major conflict

   • How is the conflict resolved?

   • Which character do you most resemble?

   • Which character do you least resemble?

   • If you played the part of that character, would this still be your favorite story?

   • Imagine the story as if it were written from a different point of view. How would you change the plot and events?

To fully understand the mythic story, imagine yourself as each of the characters in turn. Since this is your favorite tale, realize that the conflict, characters, and resolution are all resonating within your psyche.

In the archetypal layer, there are no individual events. There are only accepting principles. You usually enter this realm for the first time through a highly ritualized and charged methodology. Your reactions may range from being overwhelmed with great energy, clarity, or peace, to feeling devastated as unresolved issues confront you. By using a formal ritual of initiation in a controlled manipulation of energy, you as a member of a group are introduced to a taste of the higher levels of meditation and what can be loosely called their "higher selves." Group initiation minimizes individual negative reactions and provides a safe introduction. Nevertheless, for most people, more than one introduction is required for this realm to be integrated.

In transformative meditation, the combined identity of the energy circles allows the group to experience the introduction of the level of the archetypes with the perception of illumination by an intensely bright light. Remember how some people experienced penetrating the membrane between upper astral and lower archetypal as being similar to going through a dark tunnel? The same brilliant light that appears at the end of that tunnel parallels the description given by so many people who have had a near-death experience. Indeed, you are transcending the body-dependent realms, and beginning to experience realms where a body is not required. Since death is the event where we give up the physical body, it is easy to see how these experiences correlate in functionality and description.

While in meditation, you may inwardly perceive the brilliant golden light as you enter the archetypal layer. In ritual, you may sense astral manifestations of archetypal presences. Remember that as higher energies enter lower realms, there is an exponential increase in energy at the lower realm. Some students report seeing silvery cylinders slide down from above. To me, this appears as if someone has poured a silvery liquid into a colander that allows individual streams to pass through. For the more advanced, some of those cylinders contain the Buddha, Jesus, Tara, Mary, and almost any prominent historical or mythological figure. While these encounters may provide valuable teaching to you, there are other ongoing dynamics.

The archetypal teachers at this realm are also contained in archetypal roles. By understanding their relationships, you may also understand many karmic patterns. A human being who can hold in his or her consciousness the multiple perspectives of an archetypal pattern may use that wisdom in the mundane world. By bridging these levels of consciousness, you may create a pathway for similarly configured humans. The resolution of archetypal conflicts affects everyone who contains elements of that same archetypal identity. Your work advances the work of humanity.

Consider the mythic story of Odysseus, the hero of Troy. This man, whose adventurous nature many people share, broke pattern after his heroic successes, and instead of going home, continued his travels. You might find his adventures entertaining, but consider as well how they affected his personal life. Certainly, his wife was abandoned and left with many responsibilities of family and community. Note how easily a myth fits into everyday lives. You may find the eternal Peter Pan in your life who saddles you with all of the responsibilities. However, remember the whole story to find balancing perspectives. Odysseus is on what Joseph Campbell popularized as the "hero's journey" of transformation. You may find that as you acknowledge the archetypal roles in society, you find more meaning in life's circumstances.

You might also note that the heroic Odysseus leaves Troy with twelve ships, each containing twelve men. If you have an interest in numerology, you realize that twelve is considered a cosmic archetypal number. There are twelve signs of the zodiac, twelve hours in a day, and twelve tribes of Israel. Odysseus' journey is full of archetypal and mystical symbols.

As in all journeys of transformation, there are missteps, and Odysseus makes a few, as, inevitably, you will as well. Frequently, these circumstances provide the opportunity to learn the most. You will get different results with different groups. You may feel affinities with some archetypes and their actions and not with others. Examine them with detached interest. While it is interesting and productive to work with archetypes, for the initiate, there are higher mysteries yet to be revealed.

GROUP EXERCISE 16: EXPLORING THE ARCHETYPES

1. Ask a partner to sit in front of a blank, light-colored background. Sit facing him or her so that you can maintain eye contact. Since this exercise involves staring at someone, it may be easier for your partner to close his or her eyes. You can swap places later. As noted earlier, human vision has a built-in screen saver function of which you are scarcely aware. When you stare fixedly at a point without blinking, unchanging background begins to blank out. You might have noticed this when working at a computer for a long time. As you focus on the lit screen, the rest of the room appears to go black. You are literally experiencing tunnel vision. When you do look up, you blink several times to restore your normal vision. Consequently, when you do this exercise, try not to blink, as parts of your vision black out.

2. Find a place on your partner's face on which to focus. Continue focusing on this spot without blinking. When you are doing this correctly, parts of your partner's face will begin to morph, change shape, or even go blank. Keep your focus and just allow the process to begin.

3. Note, however, that this should not be done for more than five minutes. Your eyes can become strained and you may get an intense headache.

When this exercise is done correctly, there are several possible outcomes. Of course, the first option is that nothing happens. If you find yourself in that position, relax, then try again with a different partner in the group who has been successful. Frequently, success occurs with people you do not know very well. At the same time, staring can be considered an act of aggression in the primate world, so be sure that your partner is someone with whom you can relax later.

The more common response is that people begin to see parts of the face change. The hair may look long, and the color may be different.

Sometimes the eyes become very intense and wise, and for some, the color may change. Other partners may find that the face may change its sexual orientation as well. Be open to these experiences without judgment. The first response of the majority of people performing this exercise is to blink everything back to the configuration it normally has. Remember, don't blink (for short periods of time only).

Some people practicing this exercise suddenly become aware of auras and being able to see in the astral. They will observe light surrounding the outline of the person in front of them. These lights may be white, or any color of the visible spectrum. You may experiment with this exercise by asking your partner what his or her internal emotion was while you were "seeing." You may find correlation between your observed colors and the person's state of mind. In this way, you establish your own vocabulary between colors and emotions or thoughts.

GROUP EXERCISE 17: DETECTING HIGHER PRESENCES

Once you have achieved success in perceiving the astral realm, try Exercise 16 with a slight variation.

1. Before you begin staring, both people should meditate until firmly established in the archetypal realm.

2. Then, with subtle acknowledgment by a light touch or an opening of the eyes, you begin looking again. Find a place on your partner's face on which to focus. Continue focusing on this spot without blinking. When you are doing this correctly, parts of your partner's face will begin to morph, change shape, or even go blank. Keep your focus and just allow the process to begin.

3. You may do this simultaneously if you can maintain the archetypal clarity.

4. If working with a group, some pairs have more success than others. Allow time for at least one change of partners.

Observations may vary widely. Once, a student reported that the person in front of her turned into a monk. Another saw the Chinese goddess of compassion, Kuan Yin, in his partner. Just observe, and share your observations with your partner at the conclusion of the exercise. You may be identifying your archetypal family. Make sure that both people have the opportunity to attempt seeing in the archetypal layer. As before, you may find varying experiences with different partners. Take the time to switch partners if doing this within a group.

THE ESSENCES

After experiencing many different myths and playing many different parts, a higher perception reveals that there is only a set number of operating archetypal principles. A PBS documentary explored the idea of essences in *The Journey of Man*. Through extensive DNA analysis and exhaustive testing of the world's people, all of humanity can be traced to a tribe of bushman in Africa. The curious researcher ventured to retrace the steps of his forefathers. Arriving to this still isolated tribe, the researcher comments on how amazing it is to see all of the world's faces in such a few individuals. Indeed, you can see Asian eyes, Native American noses, and diverse traits of many peoples. Just as the DNA markers trace humanity to a single tribe with limited numbers, the archetypal energies trace back to only twelve high, pure archetypal essences.

In meditation, your encounter with the essences reveals a change in quality of intensity with or without light. A dazzling brilliant white light, frequently speckled or mottled, initially marks the realm of the essences. This stream of light particles approaches smoothly, but it is interspersed with a stream of totally black particles. These dark particles are not "an-absence-of-light" dark; rather, they are a positive black. The light is like a laser signal turning on and off very rapidly; dark is the emptiness that occurs between flashes.

At this point, it is appropriate to refine the definition of *identity*. The only thing that can move through any of these levels is identity, or the point of "I-am-ness." There can be no egoic attachments. As part of a group where strengths and weaknesses are balanced, you can move through the astral membrane because the group can reduce itself to nothing but identity. Nothing else can traverse through the membrane. Identity carries enough awareness of the nature of those things that when it reinhabits the physical body, it retains that knowing by creating codes and symbols within the brain, which provides information. However, remember that no thing can move through the barrier except identity. For this reason, all ego, physical, and mental conditioning must be transcended.

PANTHEON OF GODS AND GODDESSES

The identification of your own personal pantheon of archetypes usually emerges within your meditation experiences, or sometimes through the seeing exercises. You are profoundly changed by an experience with a pure essence. For example, I frequently found the image of the Buddha appearing during meditations in the archetypal realm. He became a marker for my entrance into the archetypal realm. With each encounter, my meditation deepened and my personality slid into the background. People soon commented that I seemed more centered and aware.

Over time, I found that Mary Magdalene, Jesus, and Kuan Yin, the goddess of compassion, frequently came with messages or insights for me. The qualities of each of these great beings became instantly recognizable. If my teacher was generating particular qualities of compassion, I could recognize the Kuan Yin aspect within him. Very few people contain only one archetypal identity; almost everyone is a mixture of three or four archetypal energies.

Had I not been working with a demanding teacher, I could have spent my life channeling messages into the world without learning of the ultimate reality. However, he reminded me of the sweet taste of illusion and encouraged me to integrate the twelve major archetypes that hold the major patterns for humanity.

Personally integrating the majority of these archetypal families is a requirement to enter the next realm of consciousness. You must enjoy and understand the lure of the Sirens in the archetypal realms, as they beckon you to study with the teachers. Continue to move forward on your hero's quest. In the transformative meditation system, you learn to rely on the direct confrontation of the energy instead of the projection of gods and goddesses. While there may be a phase of encountering teachers, divine beings, or even strange looking inorganic projections, the energy that you used to maintain a projection is now available for other uses.

GROUP EXERCISE 18: BRINGING IN THE HIGHER ARCHETYPES OR ESSENCES

1. This exercise should only be done with a group that has been practicing meditation together for several months. Most of the ego work should be well in process, and people should be able to be relatively clear of unconscious ego desires.

2. Meditate together.

3. After several moments, ask the group members to visualize a place in the room where they would like to stand for a major ritual. After five minutes or so, remind them that if it doesn't come to mind immediately, they should simply imagine a place.

4. Ask them to open their eyes, remain silent, and consciously move to the place they envisioned. Request that they hold that position until the ritual has ended.

5. The leader of the group should stand in the center. Then, through meditation, enter the highest level of energy possible. If necessary, you could ask the group to do the sandpile exercise (page 118) to generate enough energy to access the higher realms. If the leader does this correctly, then a rush of energy will permeate the body. Others in the group will have simultaneous experiences of a similar type. This energy profoundly changes people.

6. End the ritual when the energy has stopped flowing through you. Note, however, that the energy may continue to flow through others in the group. You may instruct them to remain in position as long as the energy continues to flow. Others should remain silent until everyone has completed the ritual.

7. Depending upon your group's preference, you may or may not want to discuss the effects immediately afterward.

PERSONAL ARCHETYPAL MEDITATION ACCOUNT

This meditation class was an actual event; however, the names have been changed to ensure the privacy of the individuals.

Having awakened late for meditation after a restless sleep-deprived night, I found myself drifting as the class began. I drifted right back into the dream I was having before I woke up for the day. This strange dream involved sleeping in a stone bed with high sides that should have kept me from seeing around me, yet I could see around the room—there was a soft golden light that had no obvious source. Momentarily, I was floating near the ceiling, looking down at my stone bed. Seeing my body lying there peacefully, wrapped in loose, white, linen robes, I felt so disconnected. Strangely, there was a larger bed (which looked more like a coffin) placed parallel to it. In the bed, I knew intuitively, was my father. Before I could glimpse his face, the perspective changed. Once again, I was in my body looking only straight above me. Then a man's face appeared; he was leaning over me. "Okay, you've been in there long enough," he said as he extended a hand to assist me out of the sarcophagus, for that was what it was. As I leaned forward to a sitting position, the sloping walls to the ceiling indicated that this could only be one place—the interior of the Great Pyramid. I pivoted sharply to question the man who had helped me out, but only my teacher's face greeted me. Raja's bright blue-green eyes twinkled merrily at me. I jerked back abruptly, as I remembered that the version of the teacher I knew had dark brown eyes. That paradox brought me immediately into the present, and my eyes flicked open as Raja rang the bell to end meditation.

He didn't ask for comments or questions, he just looked at me piercingly before leading the group back into meditation.

Again, it was still a dream for me. I was conscious of my father in the dream. He had died and I was part of his burial service in ancient Egypt. Simultaneously being aware of dreaming and being in meditation, I struggled to direct my dream body. I was just an observer, a conscious one, but inactive in the drama that was unfolding in my dream space. My father arises, and I attempt to communicate with him. Suddenly, the whole scene fades, as if a giant drain had been opened. That reality was swirling down the tunnel. There is a strange rushing, whirling sound, and I yelled inside the dream and meditation space, "I'm losing focus!" There was a total collapse of self as I was sucked backward out of ancient Egypt into the tunnel and awoke in this reality. Raja rang the meditation bowl, signifying the end of that sitting. My experience was over.

Others' reactions to the meditation were immediate. "Wow, that was intense," Martin offered, seemingly unable to find appropriate words beyond that while Raja waited expectantly. "I'm not sure what was going on, but I feel like I just ran a 10k race. Lots of things were going on; I just don't know exactly what."

"Me, too. There were pictures just flying by. I just can't tell you what it was like, but a lot happened," Jayne parroted.

"I don't feel right," Robert said. "I feel like I'm still floating somewhere out here."

Raja looked at him peculiarly, squinting his eyes with his head cocked at an unusual angle. "Hmm."

Then I noticed something stranger. Raja emerged from his body as an energetic double or ghostlike being and crawled to where Robert sat. His astral counterpart reached out a handlike appendage and touched the back of Robert's neck. Robert's head jerked back as if he had been touched. His eyes rolled skyward and he began to growl, much like a hurt wolf caught in a trap. He even began to drool slightly. Then he hunched over and began pawing the floor in front of him like a wild animal scratching through the ground.

"I saw what you did," I announced to Raja. He did not reply; his eyes and focus remained locked on Robert, and the physical enactment of energy manifesting through him. Robert had the look of an animal ready to chew its leg off to get free of the trap. Raja fixed his attention on Robert, who reacted violently to an unseen shock—his face contorted with white-blond eyebrows raised in horror accompanied by a mouth stretched to its limits into a horrified silent scream. Then, whether or not he shook off the seeming attack or even the channeling of an animal spirit, Robert slumped forward and let out gut-wrenching sobs. Neither Robert nor Raja offered an explanation, and no one asked. Class was dismissed for breakfast.

Chapter Eight

THE VOID

Groups generally spend months exploring the archetypes before they encounter the realm known as the Void. This level is very puzzling when you first encounter it. There is nothing to perceive—no movement, no resistance, and no thinking. You are drifting in a great space of nothingness. There is nothing you can do. There is nothing to push against, and no thinking, yet the inside of your head seems to vibrate rapidly. You are aware, but seemingly without any physical, emotional, or mental components.

The best way to describe the Void is to tell you that it reminds me of Walt Disney World's "Space Mountain" ride. In the dark, you are suddenly plunged down the roller coaster at amazing speed. There are no reference points to see where you are headed next, or to determine when the ride will end. There is no sense of personal control, and you are at the mercy of forces moving through odd twists and turns at frightening speeds. When acceleration peaks, there is a rapid change of direction, and you actually experience weightlessness—the closest analogy to the feeling inside the Void. In the dark, hurtling through space at break-neck speed with no controls or desires, you become formless, and simply exist. The Void seems empty, but paradoxically filled with an abundance of awareness.

The Void's emptiness may destroy a person who has not gone through the proper preparation, because all attachments must be given up. You must release everything that is you, otherwise you self-destruct. Extreme asceticism is one way to prevent attachments because there is less to let go of; however, it is only necessary to let go of the attachment. I have yet to experience the Void without feeling that I will be lost in it forever. Perhaps now you can begin to see the value of a good healthy foundation and a clearly defined identity. You must be pure identity to survive a foray into the Void. Consequently, most people experience the Void with a forerunner—a piece of their awareness that explores higher realms and reports back what it finds. Finding no thing in the Void, most people are quite unaware of its existence. Yet, in meditation, the forerunner is able to report an existence of a level of awareness without being able to tell you much about it. Self-deception at this stage is very easy and can prove to be a costly mistake. Entering the Void prematurely can cause extreme loss of vitality, and at the very least, a loss of interest in continuing work with a spiritual group. Better to expend more energy in ego completion and archetypal teachings than to have your illusions stripped prematurely in the Void.

GROUP EXERCISE 19: ENTERING THE VOID IN MEDITATION USING SANDPILE

1. Begin with a silent meditation. By now the group should easily reach the archetypal realm within a few minutes.

2. Let the meditation stabilize there for several minutes. You should be able to sense the state of everyone meditating together. If not, further work should be done with the archetypal realm.

3. Ring a chime or bell to ask for feedback on the meditation. Is anyone having difficulty finding the high clear space? Repeat the meditation if there are several people having problems finding the clarity in the meditation.

4. If the group has been successful, then ask everybody to return to this state of meditation. Request that everyone begin using sandpile to bring more energy and focus into the group.

5. Remind the group that there may be a transition into a new state as a result, and to remain clear and aware there. This may or may not happen the first time you attempt to cross the void.

6. You, as leader, now must wait patiently, for there is nothing you can actively do within the realm of the Void. Remain clear and wait until you sense movement that carries you through to the next membrane. After that, wait several minutes before ringing the bell to end the exercise.

7. Ask the group for feedback.

In your initial experiences there will be high drama and charged energy. Reactions may range from "I fell asleep," to "I felt like I had died." There is no sensory feedback within the Void. It is empty, but totally aware. There is very little to report from your first successful venture in exploring the Void. Indeed, you may feel that nothing at all happened. Without experience, there are few details that clue you in to the difference.

After you integrate the full spectrum of energies and find mystical clarity, you will find that the Void is better observed after you complete the entire circle of transformative meditation. Remember that all layers of awareness are not separate, but interpenetrate. When recently taking an advanced group of students through the Void, for example, I noted that it was possible to perceive there, and noted trapped souls. One of my students reported a compassionate attitude in rescuing them; may she have success in her chosen work.

If you have enough identity or are traveling through a proper ritual with a group or teacher, leaving the Void is simply a matter of waiting. Suddenly there is a sense of being drawn to something or movement arising from nothing. There is a barrier at the Void, but very few people have been able to detect it to date.

Don't mistake your experience within a ritual encounter to qualify you to do this on your own. Entry to the Void by yourself requires that you have completely stripped away all attachments in order to pass through successfully. If you attempt to this before you are properly pre-pared, you risk the acceleration of your personal, cultural, and spiritual karma. While the void may clear you of all attachments, you will pay a high price. Some unprepared people emerge totally dysfunctional afterward, finding their lives totally changed. If you have done your inner work of completing your ego and resolving your personal con-flicts, however, you will face the void and its inquisition without fear.

The Void is an all or nothing proposition. Only go there when your identity is single minded. Those who enter unprepared generally panic and fall back into astral or normal awareness. Often it will take months for them to reach the clarity necessary to attempt to traverse the Void again. The crossing of the Void is frequently compared to walking a blade's edge across the abyss. Since the results of an ill-pre-pared person can be catastrophic, this is the time that a true teacher earns his or her marks. The teacher can provide the preparation or, in the worst case, repair the damage of a premature entry.

ENTERING THE VOID

Rare individuals enter the Void of their own accord. Generally, a dra-matic push is required to enter into this realm. For some, it comes as a result of a near-death experience. For others, depression and pain lead you to the brink. For those who are healthy enough, it is usually the act of the teacher that plunges them into the abyss.

Having witnessed a few initiations within my working group, every uninitiated member has the fear that his or her turn at confrontation by me is next. The possible exceptions are those I have already con-fronted. In my own training group, my teacher did this with me, and I benefited enormously. One of my friends commented, "I'm glad it's you and not me."

Even among the best and brightest, there is a core belief around which we structure our entire lives. No one, to date, is able to disman-tle the system alone. You just can't shine the flashlight on the hand that holds it. Note that this dismantling of a core belief is not done casually. Usually it happens after someone clears most of his or her ego work. I did it heavy-handed with a student many years ago when she left the working group and moved to New York. Depending on the particular makeup of the student, I confront that person with his or her worst fear. This is usually done in private and at a time when I am sure that the student has the skills to apply to become a truer self.

Using another student as an example, Laura holds a tightly constrained belief system that she created sometime between the ages of four and six years old to protect herself from feeling everything at once. On rare occasions now, Laura is overwhelmed by her own benevolent feelings. Her fear of being exposed as being radically "different" is countered by my not doing anything to expose her. Hence, she is always waiting for the other shoe to drop. In effect, she is living in total conflict. The tension between the all-knowing, all-feeling self and the protective self that she has bound herself with is increasing. When I discussed this in circle with her, Laura's intellect had something to consider, but the unresolvable tension will also eventually expose her. Fear and intellect seesaw nicely. Knowing that there is a bear in the woods doesn't do anything to alleviate the fear! However the plunge into the abyss is accomplished, the release of this personal dynamic that rules your life catalyzes change dramatically.

GROUP EXERCISE 20: CONFRONTING YOUR INNERMOST FEARS

1. Meditate as a group until everyone has reached the level of the archetypes.

2. Ask the members to pair off with the person who knows them best, but one who isn't a spouse or significant other. Request that they sit face-to-face in close proximity.

3. Ask them to decide who will meditate first and who will ask questions. They will reverse roles later.

4. For those meditating first, ask them to find their highest and clearest meditation space and hold it throughout this exercise. They are to remain silent and simply notice when any of the questions causes them to lose awareness or focus.

5. Once the meditation is well established, the questioner begins to ask questions of the exercise partner with long pauses between each question to see if there is a loss of focus or clarity. The meditator remains silent and attempts to maintain clarity. When the person seems to be clear, go to the next question. Questions may be asked from the following list:

   · Are there any outstanding issues with your spouse?

   · Are you clear with your father? Mother? Children?

   · Are you a steady supporter of this group? This process? Your community?

   · If you could do anything you desired, what would you do?

   · Is there anything you don't want anyone to know about?

   · Who is your ideal sexual partner?

   · Are you afraid to die?

   · Have you honored your obligations? Your duties? Your work?

   · If you could go anyplace, what destination would you choose?

   · Do you love God? Do you believe in God?

   · If you could go back in time, would you change anything?

   · What is the moment when you were most happy?

   · If you could relive any moment, what would it be?

6. Ring a bell or quietly arrange a signal for the group when time is up. Let the meditators continue to meditate for another five minutes or so.

7. Reverse the roles of the partners and repeat the exercise.

GROUP EXERCISE 21: PREPARATION FOR RITUAL ENTRY INTO THE VOID

While the group may safely traverse the Void with a proven teacher, most members will not directly experience it. This is fortunate, as the unprepared person faces dire consequences such as severe loss of energy and the will to live, accelerated karmic repercussions, and possibly insanity. Careful preparation is required before a direct encounter with the Void.

To prepare the group, you may use this exercise to assist in clearing residual ego issues and personal attachments.

1. Ask the members to collectively meditate until the group identity is well established in the archetypal.

2. Ask everyone to silently remember the issues that provoked a reaction in Exercise 20, and hold the issues in the clear archetypal space of meditation.

3. Hold those issues as the group members reestablish or remember their archetypal identity.

4. Most issues easily resolve when there are no emotions to fuel them.

5. Close the circle and discuss the participants' experiences.

EXERCISE 22: ENCOUNTERING THE VOID

1. Use meditation to introduce the group to the experience of the Void. Establish the group identity in the archetypal.

2. The accomplished teacher introduces the Void by bridging all levels and sharing identity with the group. This ensures that all members pass through safely as the teacher takes on all responsibility.

3. This exercise is not recommended without an accomplished and experienced teacher.

THE TRIAD

At the boundary of the Void where you only survive as a single point of identity, you eventually arrive at a new membrane. Having passed the test of having no personal investments in this reality, you arrive at the Triad. The Triad is the pure dynamism of a trinity of forces. You may equate these to the interplay of creation, maintenance, and destruction. In many religions, the universe is described as coming into existence with the breath being maintained within the body and then being extinguished with exhalation. Regardless of how it is described, the universe is always being born, lives, and dies. The Triad reflects this process by serving as the interface between the Void and the absolute. These two worlds of undifferentiated consciousness and manifest consciousness are joined at a single point of identity. This single conscious identity catalyzes the conversion of absolute spirit into the manifest universe, and vice versa.

Accordingly, at the Triad, there are three elements always interplaying. It is the focus of consciousness that allows space-time to come into being. Consciousness determines the focus of manifestation. As in quantum physics, it is the impartial observer who determines the outcome of an experiment. Another way to look at this interface at the edge of the Void is that the Triad arrives at the moment instantly after the formation of the universe, but just before the "Big Bang." Of course, it is impossible to measure this moment since there was no time until after the Big Bang. When you arrive at the Triad during an advanced meditation, there is a physical component aware of the quantum action within the brain. You actually perceive matter and energy interchanging. Reality is always blinking.

Observing this creative act helped me finally understand Einstein's equation: energy = mass x the speed of light squared ($E = mc^2$). From my college days, I had recognized the significance of this energy/matter conversion equation, but was haunted by the qualities I could not understand. Now, finally, the pieces began to fit together in an unexpected synergy. My science background, religious interest, and meditative experience all fit together to understand creation, sustenance, and destruction in an enlightened way. Einstein's theory of relativity is a mathematical expression of the esoteric relationship and interchange between pure energy and matter. In quantum field theory, particles and their surrounding space are inseparable. Particles are interruptions in space that take form from the condensation of a continuous energy field. Particles emerge spontaneously out of the Void and disappear again within it.

Similarly, the Triad's nature is pure vitality, vitality taking form, and form dissolving. If a conscious observer quits looking at form, it would neither arise nor dissolve. The triad is simply an amorphous state neither void nor form. It isn't pure energy and it isn't form; it is a constant interplay of matter and spirit depending on the observer's focus. If you look at the substance, form materializes. You can perceive the difference between the form and the energy. Conversely, focusing on the emptiness causes the form to disappear, and by concentrating your awareness on the form, chaos diminishes. These interlinked states in the Triad take the continuous form of Ouroboros, the snake who eats his own tail. There is the maintenance of the whole that is always creating and destroying. This state is ultimately three forces comprising a whole dynamic, a trinity. The trinity of the Triad is the secret of the "three-within-one."

The boundary from Triad into the creative function is delineated during meditation with the perception of a dark sun, a phenomenon that disappears as your consciousness grows enough to encompass the truth of creating your own reality. The Triad stimulates, catalyzes, or utilizes consciousness in the creative dance of the quantum sea. This tripartite mechanism is the dynamic function that creates, maintains, and destroys the universe. In fact, the whole of creation is derived from this complex dynamic.

The quantum sea holds potential that, when exposed to the creative aspect of the Triad, begins the evolutionary spiral of life. First, minute particle elements develop into recognizable particles, then atoms form and combine into molecules or polymers that may then form simple one-celled animals. Eventually, complex matter and animal bodies evolve. This process continues indefinitely, creating all things that might be known in this universe.

All things are created from the substance or vitality of the quantum sea that permeates the universe. The Absolute is made into the substance that becomes more and more numerous, yet has less than the original vitality. In the following esoteric symbol (figure 5, "Solomon's Seal"), where the point of maximum matter is reached, there is the least spirit. Where there is infinite matter, spirit appears condensed into a point. On the other hand, if there is infinite meaning or spirit, there is only one point of matter. To understand this diagram is enlightenment in and of itself.[1]

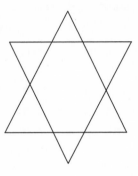

Figure 5: Solomon's Seal.

Pure spirit exists as a single point of identity that seeks materialization. Consequently, the single point of identity begins to lower its vibration. You might consider the dispersion of energy in the same way that light naturally disperses from a flashlight. The closer you hold the light to a reflecting surface, the smaller the circle is. Move the light higher, and the circle that is reflected grows larger. In two

---

1. If all matter condenses into a single point, what causes the reversal into massive expansion such as the Big Bang?

dimensions, you can illustrate that dispersion as a point that transforms into a triangle, as shown in figure 6.

Figure 6: Pure spirit descending into matter.

Simultaneously, even the densest forms of matter have consciousness. Consciousness, like helium in a balloon, seeks to ascend, so consider the point of matter transforming itself into higher realms of consciousness, and you have the following diagram (figure 7).

Figure 7: Pure matter seeking pure spirit.

The human being is the optimum vehicle for matter to achieve its goal, and conversely, for spirit to achieve manifestation. A series of esoteric symbols is derived from the combination of the two previous diagrams (figure 6 and figure 7). The optimal alignment balances matter and spirit, as shown in the resulting diagram (figure 8, page 168). This diamond shape provides a mirror image, or, as some might recognize, the image of the Great Pyramid of Giza reflected in a pool of water. In Buddhism, the achievement of the integration of realized spirit with matter results in the creation of the immortal or diamond body.

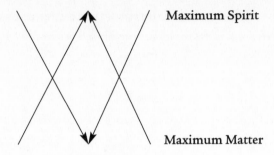

Figure 8: Matter/Spirit Interface.

In Western traditions, the familiar symbol requires the intersection of the two aspects as shown in figure 5 (page 166). Some will identify figure 5 as Solomon's Seal or the sacred six-pointed star that, in India, appears in the heart chakra. The American seal incorporates this design in the arrangement of the thirteen stars of the original colonies. You may recognize the star as a symbol depicting a realized individual— someone who has awakened mystical awareness and integrated it within the worldly body.

PERSONAL RITUAL ENCOUNTER WITH THE VOID

My teacher frequently incorporated exercises and rituals from various traditions to bring new energies and awareness in our collective consciousness. After an extensive lecture on the Tree of Life ritual that described each sephirah or station, he asked members of his group to stand in an area of their choosing. To my dismay, the one place he recommended that no one stand was the place where I was drawn. The station corresponded to the Void. In my clarity, I moved to stand with Cal in that position.

Raja looked at us curiously as his two rebel students stood back to back. He assessed our clarity and allowed us to remain in place as he began to test the pattern by running test energies through it. Cal and I leaned against each other with little expectation and some trepidation. Raja made minor adjustments in the pattern and announced that he was ready to begin transmitting energy from the highest realm. Remember that energy moving from a higher to a lower level releases an exponentially larger energy.

The immediate onslaught of energy as I faced Raja forced me to aggressively push against Cal's back. I could barely keep my footing. In a few moments, I was pushed in the opposite direction as the energy was returning from the lightning flash. Cal and I struggled to stabilize our position. Now I found myself being examined. Actually, it felt more like an inquisition. Questions of attachment demanded immediate answers. There was no time for thinking. I was stripped of all feeling, thought, emotion, and physical awareness. After realizing that I had no attachments, I was falling through dark space. I was alone and there was nothing there. Out of nothingness I recognized a huge body comprised of collections of consciousness. However, before I could observe or note anything further, the ritual was over.

Chapter Nine

THE ABSOLUTE
& MYSTICAL AWARENESS

After the experience of the Void and Triad, you emerge into the Absolute, where there is no light, but an almost indescribable brilliance. I have heard it described as an intensely brilliant black ice. There is a quality of clarity that is a visible, palpable essence with a purity that is neither light nor substance, nor anything in this universe. The Triad is best described as pure ratio or pure number, which explains why some schools promote mathematics as the purest science and expression. Certainly, the archetypal elements of numerology and the relationship as expressed in sacred geometry can be extremely enlightening.

When you approach the Absolute from the Void, you may detect what may only be called *angularity*. There are angles, certainly, but nothing that establishes that relationship, because all relationship is expressed without manifestation of form or substance.

One of my brief forays into this realm of the Absolute felt like being inside of a diamond. I felt immense clarity, and simultaneously, a strong desire arose to become matter. These moments are incredibly fleeting, but they profoundly change you. There is nothing that can truly be said that expresses the experience. There is an incredible calm, with all available knowledge and the wisdom to use it in that place. An experience with the Absolute transforms people forever. There is a change to their energy vibration. If they have completed the process of transformation, including releasing the limits of ego, there is a recognition of their divine nature within physical form. They have realized their own divinity.

I had one of those transcendent moments while teaching meditation in New York. As I made my way down the hillside, this quality glowed warmly within me. An older woman, being aided by a young woman, was headed up the path toward me, and we nodded greetings in passing. The young woman said, "You look beautiful." I quickly glanced down at the flowing dress I was wearing, and gave what seemed to be the expected reply, "Thank you." Now, having already passed me, the older woman turned and projected her voice to me, "She wasn't talking about the dress." I burst into joyous laughter.

Walking your talk sets an example of how consciousness can fully exist in the physical form. When you feel both spirit and matter equally and clearly and can become the living expression of both, you master the art of conscious living. Life becomes an experience of heaven on earth. Indeed, the illusions of separation disappear. Heaven and earth become the same thing. Every duality becomes a different expression of the same thing. The illusions of existence and nonexistence disappear. A noticeable sense of joy permeates your being.

Unfortunately, you probably cannot hold that level of awareness all the time. However, having once achieved it, you can strive to attain it again. The dynamics of dualism in our real lives frequently call us into learning situations. Earthly existence is one of learning relationships. You, as a wise person, must learn to be in this world and not be of it. This is the dance of enlightenment.

Being in the world is the ultimate challenge for the enlightened person. In my own life, I found that I longed for a monastic life. Yet, each time I reached the level of achievement that satisfied my teachers, I was told, "Your work is not on the mountaintop. Your work is down in the world." There is no preaching to the choir allowed. The real work lies in transforming the matter of this world. With the trials of terrorism, pollution, overpopulation, and diseases such as AIDS, cancer, and diabetes, there is work for everyone who is willing. Even small, seemingly random acts of kindness make vital differences in the consciousness of this world. Working consciously together and creating dialogues for understanding evolve greater awareness of the interconnectedness of all life.

THE GURU

For those who may master the spectrum of consciousness and the energy transformations required in them, you may become a guru and teacher to others. Relatively few individuals span the entire spectrum, and fewer still are qualified to teach it. Ultimately, gurus span the entire spectrum of consciousness and are functional in all levels of awareness. For example, in the dream state, gurus are not only aware while asleep, but are also in control of their astral body and can manipulate it appropriately. Having entwined energies with their students, they become dreamweavers as they connect conscious and unconscious threads in the working group members' lives. When a student is caught in emotional turmoil, the guru frequently dreams the identical dream. If the student has requested help in this drama, the guru can change the astral dynamics to reveal the underlying issues. Many personal dynamics can be resolved in the dream level without having to suffer so much turmoil in the waking state. Connecting through the astral realms allows major shifts in awareness.

While gurus have a major presence in the astral realm, there is a highly developed expression of identity in all realms of consciousness. Therefore, gurus consciously animate one level for students to sense those qualities while bridging the paths to the next. This ability to animate and bridge is an inherent quality to true identity; therefore, the guru's nature becomes the structure in transformative meditation. Meditation that includes visualization of gurus, tantric deities, or gods and goddesses rely on this identification to bridge to higher levels of awareness.

When I successfully span several levels, the by-product of energy is enormous since a higher vibration can be transmitted to a lower one. On occasion, there is so much energy that the hairs on my arms stand on end. There is an outpouring of benevolent energy and consciousness, which infiltrates the boundaries of this space-time and this body. Within an energy circle, this causes people to lean backward, feel heat, or feel an incredible presence. Actually, only a tiny fraction of the energy passes back and forth between levels. A guru's embodied consciousness can span these levels simultaneously, and share the energies to allow others to be introduced to them. Be nice to the gurus; they are extremely rare people. The guru's structure becomes your ladder and guiding principle.

While reading this book provides the basic structure of the transformative meditation spectrum, to *realize* the work requires practice. One of the most efficient ways to comprehend the interaction of consciousness and matter is to work with groups who experience them. Some of my students teach introductory circles throughout the world and are well versed and competent to demonstrate these techniques for you. While you may learn many of these techniques by starting your own group, mentoring with an established lineage teacher will give you confidence and validation in your work.

The collective meditation technique we utilize allows a group of people, acting as a single unit with their guru, to experience each level. By practicing group meditation, eventually you retain memory of the experience of these places. With enough drive, clarity, and experience, you become conscious and functional in higher realms. You begin establishing identity in realms that alone you would not be able to access. Once functional there, you may simply remember that feeling and find that clarity again when working alone. At that point, you are establishing your own identity. By returning to an established group and attempting to share your experience, the group's reflections will tell you whether you are successful or caught in an illusion. This is a valuable asset in working with established circles. Integration at higher levels of consciousness is a difficult but extremely rewarding journey. Your group reflects you until you no longer need its reflection to realize who and what you are.

There is another advantage in continuing work with a group. Shared experiences allow the group members to remember their combined identity and achieve the higher realms of consciousness more easily. In my own working group, I have difficulty finding the lower realms since we skip over them so quickly. In fact, I frequently add new people to the group so that I can continue to demonstrate the lower realms of awareness. A side benefit to changing the makeup of the group is that the process of learning continues. More advanced students can now observe the earlier dynamics from a higher perspective and may uncover the mechanics to teach others. Therefore, the learning process is passed on to others who in turn will continue to evolve consciousness. Group dynamics in any organization can be both beneficial and frustrating, yet everything proves worthwhile when you see a light bulb turn on for someone.

With enough practice, you can use the group for your own benefit. By sharing identity, you can simply remember a certain realm you've experienced and you will immediately arrive there. If you have established a toehold of identity, you may remember all that has ever consciously occurred on that realm in your existence. This may be useful to recall information in your past, process any unresolved issues, or to understand finer points of relationship. In many cases, your past is the best predictor of your future. Of course, the whole point of becoming more conscious is to change patterns and enhance life.

If you are able to complete the transformative spectrum of consciousness, you may remain fully aware in the body and link all the levels of existence from the cells up. The goal of highly enlightened beings is to unify all the levels of awareness. In doing so, you resolve all duality, which is no small matter. You must ultimately unify the identity, sexuality, judgment, and separation from others. When you are energetically whole and there are no blockages between the functional levels of being, you are an integrated being who no longer segments awareness into specialized tasks. Higher consciousness allows you to function harmoniously in all realms. The completed human being, enlightened in the body, thinks, feels, is, knows, and creates. Every action is sensual, wise, and has motives that are linked to others. A completed human says fearlessly what he or she feels, thinks, and knows, and can communicate all of these things. The super person is unified. The real task lies in unifying all of reality. If you are able to complete the great circle of transformative meditation, then you will find yourself in a position to change the world.

ENTERING NEW REALMS Of MEDITATION

In the transition from energy circles to energy within meditation, there are some nuances that you should know. When you first enter a new realm in meditation, the most direct form of enlightenment consists of consuming the qualities of that level. Rather than experiencing these realms through the use of clairvoyance or clairsentience, you go directly into the core of transformative energy. This core is frequently described as a shaft or channel that the group awareness uses to access higher energy within the working circles. This is a normal result of an esoteric combining of group energy that creates a direct energetic core comprised of almost total essence and total vitality.

You might find a comparison of this central core vitality and your use of it helpful. For example, consider that the core shaft of energy is an elevator, while the floors are the various higher realms. The different states of consciousness and the different levels of reality are to be found only when you step out of the elevator. The car is the vehicle taking you up and down this particular department store of consciousness, while the guru is the elevator operator.

If you enter the elevator, you inevitably move. Similarly, when you are in the central core of energy, you immediately charge or fill the body with chi. If you remain focused, you may sense rising. This is the bodily reaction attempting to cope with a sensation that it is not conditioned to interpret. If you become distracted or fearful, you may lose enough focus so that you are no longer in the central core. The energy may be lost and you may lose the benefit of the group energy for further exploration.

By staying within the core, the energy provides the opportunity to discover new realms of awareness. When you encounter a new level, there are three potential ways to experience it. First, there is the direct energetic perception. Generally, that experience is limited to those who have fully integrated a realm. Second, to some spiritual explorers, the new realm is frequently experienced as the manifestation of the energy at that level. You might detect it as the release of energetic bubbles. The third way is to be so far removed from the manifestation as to be able to objectively look at it, see it, and describe it. These stages are not equal, but identical to each other. The perspective is different due to the individual development of inner essence. This is a trinity of observation, manifestation, and inner burning vitality on each defined realm of consciousness.

MEDITATION AND MYSTICISM

One goal of transformation is to transcend the need to leave the body in order to experience the Absolute, and instead integrate it within a healthy, complete human being. Life is filled with abundance of joyous spirit. In this combination, you can access primal vitality, chi, and fill your cup until it overflows. This powerful symbol is used in the traditional tarot deck in several cards with liquid flowing continuously. When there is more vital essence than is needed, the spillover energizes all of those around. Abundance of energy is key to maintain a full capacity of vitality since it is what must be used to build identity. This is of vital importance to healers. Healing others should be done from excess vitality and not from personal levels. There is also an enhanced quality of sharing from a place of abundance rather than from your own vitality. Fill your cup first, and then serve the world from abundance.

The transformed human being, sharing completely in spirit and form, will encounter time in a different way. You become sensitized enough to notice this distinction. When time is encountered directly, all separateness disappears. Rather than having a compassionate acceptance of others, you become simultaneously existing in all things. All other beings are an extension of you instead of an intellectual choice to lower the barriers of the ego self. When time is transcended, there is no choice to accept others since there are no others. There is no choice to love everyone; there is no one else. There is only self. Separation is only possible when you believe in the artificial construct of time.

Time, though an artificial tool, can't simply be abandoned. Time serves the important function to separate the events of a life or lives. While the mystic may see all events happening at once, time differentiates the functioning consensual reality from other ones. This also explains why functional mystics see events throughout time so readily. They may simply choose which time period to experience.

You, as an advanced initiate, can go out of this reality into an alternative one with relative ease. Awareness of reality is not linear except by our choice. For an analogy, an old motion picture is projected at sixteen frames per second, but the mind interprets the flow of frames as continuous motion. Observed closely, the film flickers. (Currently, film speed is doubled and the flicker is almost undetectable.) If you detect this flicker, it provides an obvious clue that the film reality is not continuous. If you note other anomalies, such as wheels turning backward, then we have clues to the illusionary nature of the film. For example, taking a closer look at the backward turning wheels reveals how perception creates reality. Remember that the speed at which film frames are taken is not synchronous with the spinning wheels. Imagine a chalk line drawn on the tire radius in the twelve o'clock position. The tire rotates at a certain speed; for simplicity, let's say at 1 revolution per second (1 rps). A timing light can by synchronized to take a picture once every second. Since the speeds of the picture taking and tire rotation are matched, each picture frame reveals the mark in the vertical position. However, in shooting television or motion pictures the speed of the picture taking is fixed at a constant while the tire speed is variable. While the chalk line may be at noon initially, the next frame shot reveals the line at nine o'clock. The next frame shows the line at six o'clock. In our example, the tire moves clockwise nine hour marks in each frame. Yet, the series of photographs reveals a snapshot that shows a line that is moving backward three hours each time. Such is the nature of illusion.

Similarly, consensual reality offers clues to its nature as well. A conscious person has control of the choice of which reality to experience and can be considered a functional mystic. Without the ability to control the choice of reality, you might experience a life similar to Billy Pilgrim, who time-trips through *Slaughterhouse-Five* with no control over his experiences. Billy Pilgrim finds himself in a different reality several times a day. His predicament includes being one-half of an exhibit in a zoo on the planet Tralfamadore; the other half is an exotic dancer who had disappeared from earth years before. Billy is living a fantasy world on earth when viewed from his other reality. Such people in our reality frequently end up in mental hospitals.

Reality is, however, always flickering. When the flicker is observed, reality is known not to be constant. In films, you choose to focus on the pictures instead of the blank places separating the pictures. The focus on the discontinuities is the secret of experiencing life beyond normal perception. Normally, your identity processes the selection of connected events to form a continuity of a particular nature. The mystic realizes that total reality is an experience of all things happening at the same time, at the same place, collapsed. Instead of viewing a film frame-by-frame, for example, you can pick up the film canisters and know the entire plot.

For the functional mystic, all worlds, all times, and all perspectives are available. As shown in figure 9 (page 180), which resembles an apple core, the mystic is in the center with different time lines extending out in space and returning to the center. Experiencing a perspective is simply a matter

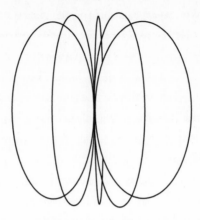

Figure 9: Apple core of time-loops.

of choice. I refer to these lines as time-loops because they are cycles of experience that can only be escaped once you meet the criteria. When you have mystical awareness, all of these do-loops are available to you. For the mystic, there is a bridging of lives and accumulated wisdom to bring to the reality where the physical body resides. While multiple realities may coexist, the physical body grounds the mystic to the realm where expression is possible.

The ultimate goal of the transformative meditation process is to train you to negotiate the perception of different states, then to allow the perception to include all of the spaces at once. This ability is not foreign to you. You have mystical flashes all the time that are immediately forgotten. A mystical flash is not just a higher reality, but also an opening of what appears to be continuity into a place where you may select and negotiate a number of different realities. Remember the wheels turning backward in the movie? This is a flash of a higher reality intruding onto a lower one. If you pay attention to the anomalies in consensual reality, you will create an opening to learn about a higher operating system that determines it.

In the case of film projection, it is the persistence of memory that makes a motion picture work. By holding the image of one frame until the next one appears, your mind generates continuity. By the way, there is a movement reflecting the fast pace of our society. There is a proposal to compress voices on the radio. A computer will analyze the voice tapes and eliminate any overtly long pauses, hums, or random spaces. The messages will be compressed, and there will be more meaning in less time. The obsession with time marks our increasing awareness of it.

A mystical experience transcends time. There is awareness of being out of this reality, out of limited perception, and into a realm that embraces more than your actions and who you were at that time. One of my most dramatic mystical experiences happened during a visit to Stonehenge. On a whim, instead of going home for Thanksgiving, I hopped on a jet headed to London. Without any advance planning, I simply left on my adventure. The great challenge for me was to take care of myself in the moment. I was traveling to another country without even having a reservation for a place to stay upon arrival.

My first night in London I took in the latest Andrew Lloyd Webber production. The next day I drove out to Stonehenge since I had always been a fan of the King Arthur myths and the magic associated there. However, when I arrived at the cow pasture containing the stones, I felt nothing and was extremely disappointed. The stones were fenced off and tourists were kept from the circle. Since it got dark very early in November, I returned to the nearby town for lodging and a meal.

After dinner, the full moon was rising and I returned to Stonehenge in hopes there would be magic. Again, I was disappointed to find only the solitude, and returned to the inn. Before falling asleep, I prayed to whatever guides I thought might help me clarify the ongoing but troubling romantic relationship I had with a man named James. The response was immediate. Several imaginary movie projectors turned on simultaneously in the panoramic theater of my room, making it extremely difficult to focus on any particular one. However, each "film" contained the same cast in different times and places. As soon as I recognized James and me in the cast of one picture, a new film would replace it. I saw us as black brothers walking barefoot in the plains of Africa. Then that scene faded into one where we were members of a royal court in medieval England. Another film attracted my interest, and I saw us as grain sellers in the market of Pompeii. I kept seeing lifetime after lifetime with this man, and it appeared we always had a great deal of affection for each other. Now I began to understand my feelings for James. We had a series of past lifetimes together that provided memories of our relationship in this lifetime.

Years afterward, I began to understand what occurred at Stonehenge. With a more fully developed identity, I learned to access the mystical realm where this Stonehenge event had happened. Over time, I have reached this mystical realm where time and space have no meaning. Every time there, I remember other visits I've made as well. There is a vast knowledge stored within that identity that remains hidden almost all the time. Sometimes glimmers from that perspective appear in my consciousness when seeing new landscapes in film, or a passage in a book stimulates that often unachievable space.

Without enough identity in previous visits, however, as soon as I left that space, the experiences were promptly forgotten. With practice, I learned to retain the memories of these mystical experiences. Soon I was able to string them together where I found an alternative self. Instead of forgetting who I was in these events, I developed a memory of existing in these alternative conditions and remembered both states. The higher state has no problem remembering who I am in the mundane world, but the mundane self often did not remember who I was in the higher one. Specific mystical development and memory was necessary before the two were integrated within my consciousness.

According to Greek mythology, memory is an important gift from the goddess Mnemosyne, daughter of heaven and earth. Memory allows experience and resultant wisdom, since you may learn from remembered events. Without it, you are continually facing each day anew and survival itself becomes a challenge. However, consider the possibility that you may remember beyond the events of this lifetime. Suppose you have the power to remember the theme and purpose of each incarnation and the reason you chose to be reborn this time. Imagine how much spiritual work you could accomplish! This ability is well within your capability. The mystical state allows time itself to be manipulated. There is no longer separation between these selves; they are concurrent selves. All memory and wisdom of previous lives may be brought to your awareness in your current body. You transcend time when you are functional in the mystical state. The persistence of memory is a major factor in becoming conscious, while transcendence of time is a major factor in becoming a functional mystic.

The highest level that human beings can pick up is the level of the Higher Archetypes, or twelve fundamental essences. Here, the planetary and universal energies push the level of human consciousness' ability to perceive. Beyond the Higher Archetypes lies the Void. Some conditions that have been reported are that there is a direct conscious experience of being dead without the morbidity, and that there is an emptiness of everything other than consciousness. The Void can be equated to trying to read a book in a pitch-black room. You read nothing, but it is not an empty space. There is no content. The Absolute encompasses pure content. Within the enlightened human being, there remains the awareness within all being.

THE MYSTICAL STATE

All successful meditation leads to the mystical state. Mystics are people who remain conscious of these states. While drugs, trauma, migraines, and synergy may all provide transitory states of mysticism, the mystic lives in them.

Precursors of a mystical experience include an awareness of a bright, radiant light, perhaps the viscosity of the air seems thicker, and time itself seems suspended. These moments seem magical, yet almost all of us have had periods of mystical awareness. In the highly charged states of dance, sexual pleasure, or even watering the garden, there is a combined state of high awareness that seems adrenaline charged. You not only feel a heightening of the senses, but you feel exalted. Along with this exaltation you feel an incredible calm, peace, and inexplicable joy.

There are three minor exercises that can be used to expose you to the possibilities of the mystical state.

Micro-Movements

Try moving your hand as slowly as possible. As you barely move, you will note a shift in the muscles. The long striated muscle can no longer maintain the muscles' smooth movement. The motion becomes a series of small jerks. In those jerks resembling frames of film, there are moments of mystical experiences.

Observing a Pendulum

A pendulum, a weight swung from a fixed point by a line, traces an arc along the bottom. Notice what happens when it changes direction. There is a pause that cannot be mathematically defined. For an instant, the pendulum is outside of this space-time. If your meditation skills allow it, you may observe a break in consensual reality.

Alternately, this same cyclic reversal of direction occurs at every breath. When your breath changes from an inhalation to an exhalation, there is a timeless moment of stillness. Holding your breath for short intervals may enhance your awareness of this mystical moment.

Detecting the Flicker of a Light Bulb

Using a very low wattage light bulb (15 watts or less), try staring at the light without blinking. If you can detect the flicker of light within the bulb (60 Hz), you may also note that the filament glows continuously. You ignore this all the time. This exercise is useful in learning how to adjust your mind to detect other realms. You're constantly selecting different bands of awareness.

A PERSONAL MYSTICAL MOMENT

In my meditative version of a pure land, a vast matrix of interconnected crystals shines in an otherwise dark field of black clarity. Only a pure being who achieves the functional mystic level has the creative ability to form a crystal. These interlinked crystals are fixed patterns that continue to evolve consciousness by interacting within this reality. Each crystal contains the seed for an individual/planetary reality.

As I made this observation, I realized that the matrix of linked crystals represented masculine aspects of the Creator.

My awareness deepened and the center of the earth opened to reveal a twelve-sided iron crystal at its center. Intuitively, I knew that this was the feminine aspect of the Creator. By combining the masculine and feminine, a new world is born. This level of awareness was incredible—absolutely pure. There was no sense of time, but I began feeling the need to return to my body awareness. Suddenly, stars came into view in the deep recesses of space. They resembled the huge light-emitting crystals. Recognizing the patterns of stars against the dark background, I knew I could find my way back home.

With a rush, I was drawn into a dark crystal. There was nothing there but awareness. All I desired was to be in form—to be human. Then, suddenly, double doors opened out of the darkness and I found my astral self in Reynolds Hall, the meeting place of one of my groups. I was alone, but the meeting room was filled with golden light. I brought that energy down into the physical to return to an enlightened state in the physical body.

GROUP MIND: ENERGY, TRANSFORMATION, AND MEDITATION

At levels just above and just below ordinary awareness, there is the possibility of linking consciousness together to create a single mind composed of many individuals. There are several good reasons for the creation of a group mind. First, it may provide assistance to expedite the process of attaining higher awareness for the learning meditator. Second, by consciously combining individuals into a single group, an individual's weaknesses may be countered by other individuals' strengths. As a functional member of a working meditation group, members may experience new awareness unavailable to them individually. Eventually, the group forms a single body with more clarity and insight than any individual. The whole becomes greater than the sum of its parts. Finally, as the group progresses, it may serve as a working blueprint for humanity. There has always been a collective consciousness, but humanity has not become fully aware of it. When we do rise to the occasion, humanity will assume a more active role in the evolution of consciousness.

Note that the linking of higher consciousness is most effective above the transpersonal level. While individuals within the group may take on archetypal roles, the combined identity of the group itself becomes integrated in higher mystical realms. This organization at the transpersonal level causes a shift in focus from the individual mind toward a view of a collective mind of humanity, where the visionary capacity of human awareness is limitless.

In the linked archetypal patterns of group consciousness, the traditional wisdom of the past shapes patterns for the future. When history repeats itself, everything comes full circle. With each completion of a cycle, however, time has marched on in a linear fashion. The circle is stretched out through time, resembling a continuing spiral of evolution. With each repetition of our past, we have the opportunity to apply the acquired wisdom of our experiences and change the future. In the present moment, we are unraveling the past, being in the now, and creating a new vision of the world.

Unraveling our past is a complex procedure. While each of us has a specific calling or mission that we revere, there is also our need for healthy community, loving relationships, and creative outlets. Our cultures, history, and ancestry have shaped boundaries that may impair a global vision. Only with the destruction of static patterns do we release the old to make room for the new. For many members who have attained functionality in the mystical realm, they are already unraveling the karma of this time.

For example, Velda writes to me from Germany:

> I am forwarding my e-mail to this forum. Doing so helps me to face my fear of rejection, not fitting in, etc. It is scary to be different and experience things others do not. I am safe . . . I am safe . . . I am safe . . . Monday evening I found myself in a small alcove by

the river. As I started to leave the alcove, I felt a barrier and saw faeries as guards to the alcove. I got the impression they wanted me to stay, so I went back into the alcove and immediately "jumped through a hoop" to a different dimension. I could feel Herzo behind me as a medieval town, I could feel the Knights of Nurnberg and _____ (I originally wrote Herzo, but I don't think this is correct) on the meadow. I could see it all as something like a shadow; however, the modern events were there as well. I left the alcove and walked in 2 worlds for a while; the smell of olive trees was heavy in the air. It made my heart ache for home (where I grew up and my mom still lives), but I heard a voice say, "No. This is much more ancient." I suppose at this time, I should tell you that I am being beckoned by Green Goddess energy. In the past, I have rejected that as well as any other energy on that level because I didn't want to get stuck "playing" on that level, as it is my desire to go past that to the "Source." I have also rejected traveling to other dimensions, faeries, etc., as it seemed to have no real purpose other than to play. I mean what purpose could it possibly serve to see Herzo in the 1300s, the revolutionary war, etc.? Writing in my journal, I realized I have been jumping through the hoop since I was a child. I always believed it was because I had a special tie to the place in which I was living at the time; however, now I wonder if it was because of special ties or just because that is who I am and what I do.

Why does the jumping experience bring with it such longing sorrow to the heart and solar plexus chakras? Is this a necessary step on the path of masterhood? It seems that most masters I know of jumped quite often. Why do they have this ability? Did they feel the sorrow? And must I feel so nauseous when I even think about this? Or is it because I am missing something, resisting the experience? What is the purpose of jumping, seeing other dimensions, etc.? I am not clear on this yet, but still seeking answers.

I answered Velda with the explanation that she may be visiting the alternate reality of Herzo to unravel the karma entanglement there. As an aware, linked, and capable mystic, Velda had always been capable of jumping through the dimensional hoop and contributing the "Great

Work." She could elect to be a part of that reality as well as remaining functional in this one. By connection with the Green Goddess energy, she could examine all the dimensions where she embraced or rejected that energy. Her patterns throughout lifetimes were revealed as she integrated her archetypal energy.

As to the longing, I can empathize with Velda. When reconnecting to an energy that matches your "soul," all the dimensions open and, ever so briefly, you are reunited with the divine. Why would you resist such a momentous event? Well, consider the pain of returning to the "real" world, the responsibility of knowing your work on this physical plane and possibly not being able to remain firmly entrenched within this reality. Uncontrolled forays into this type of experience can be slightly disturbing! However, the group provides karmic weight to firmly establish your connection to the physical body. Eventually, all group members may bridge two worlds. In the meantime, your human body may be reacting with nausea to attempt to prevent you from doing this. The animal nature of the body likes the illusion that it is in charge. It's not; you are more than your body. The longing for that divine union is all-consuming. Tell your body you're not going to abandon it, which is its fear. Entry into the Absolute offers an intriguing paradox; there is a choice to return to the physical realm or to merge into the divine. Masters have the ability to clear karma by bridging worlds. Fundamentally, however, clearing karma is part of the evolution of consciousness.

PERSONAL AND COLLECTIVE MEDITATION EXERCISE

1. This exercise can be done alone or with the group; the results should be the same. Invoke the energetic connection to the group through chant, calling its name, or simply remembering its presence.

2. Find your center and allow the energy to flow down into the body.

3. As your meditation deepens, recall a member of the group. Hold the memory of his or her face in your awareness. Often you will

sense his or her state of mind. Just feel the connection between you for a few moments, and then let go.

4. Repeat step 3 for every member of the group.

5. Allow the memory of the entire group sitting together to rise in your consciousness. Feel the energy as it combines and moves through your body.

6. Offer your love and energy to the collective, and end your meditation.

THE RISE AND FALL OF CONSCIOUS CIVILIZATIONS

In many religions and myths, there is the destruction of one way of being before another mode is born. Death, living, and rebirth form cycles of existences. The preservation of humanity on earth will require letting go of our materialistic worldview in order to form a more flexible, harmonious relationship in our world. In humanity's subconscious lies the mythical place of Atlantis. This highly technically advanced civilization was an experiment of placing high consciousness in dense matter. To facilitate this, large crystals were planted in the earth, creating energetic ley lines to shift the life forces on the planet. These long ley lines crisscrossed the earth in a matrix of creative energy. Unfortunately, the corruption of power over other species resulted in the destruction of the Atlantean civilization and the energetic crystal matrix.

If, indeed, history repeats itself, we are in a place very similar to the mythic technology-based Atlanteans. In the present moment, our highly dependent technology-based life exists at a high price to the environment and third world countries. Rather than continuing to live in incongruous ways, we must find a communal egoism and synthesize a new vision of harmonious coexistence. We cannot return to the past or hold the illusions of a dying way of life. We must act as one or face our own destructive end. Hopefully we bring more wisdom and higher awareness to this turn of the spiral.

While individuals may hold separate visions of the world, as a conscious group we are able to integrate diverse ideas and find a common worldview. I am reminded of this during Children's Week at a retreat center. Worlds exist within worlds. At the moment outside my window, there is an imaginary world full of knights, sorcerers, and princesses created by a children's adventure game. As I walk through their midst on the way to the hilltop sanctuary where I teach meditation, they take no notice of me. I do not exist in their reality. Within a nearby classroom, a Native American elder chants a song of renewal. Each of us is carefully contained in our bubble of consciousness, yet we are united in an overseeing administrative structure that gave form to that special week. Even that structure is simply a bubble in another version of a larger reality. Our consciousness can expand by linking to the similarities and threads than run through all realities. Without judgment, we find higher identity and reality that links all life together. Within that worldview, we still own our center while functioning harmoniously within the larger whole. From the axis mundi, the central axis from which all realities of this world originate, a new world vision is created with clarity and sensitivity.

While individuals in transformative meditation groups learn to embrace the collective higher consciousness, they must also express this higher consciousness within their daily lives. For a new world vision to emerge, we must develop higher awareness in every aspect of our lives. We must become aware of the dreams, myths, and mystical perceptions. We must cultivate the skills, talents, and abilities of higher awareness. With every person we meet, consciously or unconsciously, we are weaving a web of connectivity. If we hold a global vision, our deeds and spirit are shared in everyday actions. As the cycles of the past predict all too well a chaotic future, we must respond with a common goal. The future of our human race is at stake.

The time for transformation and awakening is now. This system of transformative meditation teaches practitioners to develop a non-egoic identity that holds an ethical concern for life in all forms. Through shared viewpoints within a working group, we reaffirm our places within the world and imbue them with higher meaning. We learn to communicate first with each other, and then to transmit this vision to others. The relationship to the whole determines the degree to which this message is received. There is a constant refining as we wear away prejudice and bias. Well-established and accomplished groups serve as experimental models in shaping the transition that humanity faces.

Our evolution through billions of cycles, acknowledged or unseen, calls for a shared vitality and union of all life. We cannot reach full potential without becoming aware of the transformation of energy in all forms. Our duty is to value all species, all life, and all consciousness in this increasingly fragile ecosystem. As humanity has caused the demise of some species, we must assume the karmic responsibility for the act of transforming energy at that level. The human form is the most capable of transforming complex energies. When we consume plants, we are also assuming their transformation of light, water, and earth into a higher vibratory physical form. When we eat meat, we are consuming not only the animals' transformation of plant energy into animal fuel, but also its food that includes the plant's photosynthesis process. Our world is built on transforming energies into higher and higher consciousness. The strands of consciousness that connect all life weave the fabric for existence.

The primary challenge for humanity is to awaken to all dimensions of awareness. They have always surrounded us, and now we must learn to recognize the mystical and mysterious sea of awareness. In forming groups of enlightened individuals, we open our hearts to the full depth of being. As illusions dissolve, we find the sacred illuminating all life. Through this system of transformation through meditation, we realize our true potential and gain knowledge and power to contribute to a new world vision.

More and more of these types of evolved groups may link together in these higher and lower realms to hold positions similar to the shining jewels reflecting each other in Indra's net. The net is formed by the intersection of the lines of space and time, and this lattice holds the transformative energies that infuse creation. Like the reflecting jewels or stars shining in space, conscious rays of light shift the lines of consciousness engaged in this reality. In this way, consciousness shapes reality. On my first trip to Egypt, I felt a karmic obligation to open a portal to an ancient system of wisdom despite my personal challenges. Yet through an incredible chain of events, I found myself in the desert sands in Saqqara, Egypt, performing an ancient diamond body ritual with two shamanesses. The energetic ultraviolet web surrounding this planet revealed itself as faces, modern and ancient, to form crystals at each intersection of lines. Then, for the first time in eons, one of the crystals created light from within, and its rays shone along its lines of connectivity. These rays then transmitted the creative fire to each crystal that in turn began to light up. Suddenly, I again had hope that humanity would be enlightened in time to create a supportive role for our host planet.

THE X-POSITION EXERCISE

By now the working meditation group should look forward to energy circles and simple rituals. While some people will not be conscious of the work in its entirety, by loaning their physical and higher energies they will share in the mystical awareness of the group. I introduced my first working group to the "Great Work" during an outdoor ritual in the Georgia countryside.

1. Form a large circle with exaggerated spaces between people.

2. Ask the group members to create a large X out of their body by holding their hands up to the sky and their legs spread apart as a mirror reflection to the earth.

3. Each person is to experiment with the position until he or she finds a flow of energy from the top of the body flowing to the ground. In doing so, the group collectively holds enough energy to

open personal barriers to the mystical realm. These moments are fleeting.

4. Ask the group not to speak after rituals, but to hold on to those moments.

5. After some moments, begin to share the thoughts, feelings, and experiences of the ritual in order to fully understand it. In this way, the opening to higher consciousness allows a downward flow into the earthly plane. Within the human body, the transformation of energy rises from the earth and descends from the heavens to enlighten the heart.

THE NEW WORLD VISION

The future of humanity requires adaptation to ensure its survival. We must change our destructive materialistic ways and protect the place that gives us life. Through enlightened groups, we must create a new world vision. A developing collective mind recognizes no borders, no political loyalties, no cultural prejudices. There is only one planet and one race—earth and the human race. Transformative meditation groups serve as pathways to bring more people into awareness of the global mind. The global mind has always existed; however, humanity has not been conscious of it.

Transformative meditation provides tools and techniques to evolve humanity into becoming conscious of its place within the universe. Instead of deadening our awareness to our environmental plight, the deadly diseases that threaten us, or the ethics of scientific advancement in cloning, gene therapy, and stem cell research, we must become more aware. We must feel every sorrow, every joy, and the whole range of divine expression on this planet. Our education must include global concerns and relationships. Only then can we understand the massive nervous system of this planet and act in accordance to a global vision. The root of our existence lies with the ability to evolve and adapt in harmony with our host.

Like the entangled root system of a giant forest of aspen trees or a school of fish that swims as one body, we must learn to function as one unified being. The first step is to educate us on our role within this ecosystem. In the Gaia concept, this planet is one ecological system in which humanity has become the most destructive force. The conscious natural selection to change how we affect the planet is within our own power by developing higher awareness. We must balance reason and intuition, right brain and left brain, the computer wizard and the portrait artist. Duality is in a dance with unity.

Any system that brings a person to this group mind identity is valid because in the final goal, there is only a single consciousness. Whether it is Sufi dancers spinning the forces of the universe, monks contemplating koans, or transformative energy groups, our culture must create the neural connections of pure awareness. We must do the work wherever we are, doing whatever we do. Our animal nature and spiritual self may coexist in harmony. Humanity's effect on the planet must be balanced with the forces of awareness to reshape our place into a harmonious relationship. As enlightened human beings, we may join forces with other enlightened beings to promote the education in global awareness.

The issue of enlightened minds transcends issues of religion as well. The work of transforming consciousness cannot be left to the dedicated monks, nuns, priests, or priestesses. The adaptive work must not remain in the ashrams and churches; it must become the responsibility of every individual. As a spiritual initiate, you must become aware of the higher realms of consciousness that are humanity's birthright.

From tribal villages to global and even universal neighborhoods, humanity must expand its concepts to embrace a collective consciousness. There are infinite possibilities. As we comprehend the myriad complexity of both our inner and outer worlds with the remembered experience of all our pasts, enlightened minds become a conscious force that shape our world. Combined at highest levels of awareness, humanity then may finally achieve its destiny as conscious cocreators.

We shall not cease from exploration
And the end of all our exploring
Will be to arrive where we started
And know the place for the first time.

—T. S. Eliot

GLOSSARY

Absolute

The highest realm of consciousness. Marked by brilliance beyond the capabilities of the human to perceive directly.

Amitabha

The Buddha most often associated with the Pure Land School of Buddhism practiced in Japan.

Arcanum

Vow of silence required by the mystery schools regarding their secrets. Breaking the arcanum was punishable by death.

Archetype

Energetic principles forming the universal patterns of manifestation.

Asana

Yoga postures that open the body to higher realms of consciousness.

Asleep

An esoteric meaning that someone is living without any higher awareness. To a conscious being, these people appear to be sleepwalking through life.

Astral

Realm of consciousness encompassing sleep, dream, healing, and magical states. Comprised of the emotional fluid, the astral is marked by vivid colors, dream bodies, and feelings.

Astral Travel

The ability to use the dream body to visit other places and times.

Atman

From the Hindu religion, a term for individualized consciousness.

Aura

The energetic field interpenetrating matter. Many clairvoyants see these striations of energy as colors around the physical form.

Avatar

A realized human being who holds the quality of a pure archetypal principle or essence.

Awake

In esoteric meaning, this means to be conscious and aware of higher realms of consciousness while being involved in the real world.

Black Hole

Spherical region of space containing a gigantic gravitational field so large that everything is attracted to it, and nothing, not even light, escapes from it.

Bodhisattva

Being who forgoes total enlightenment in order to assist all sentient beings in achieving it.

Boundary

A well-defined limit of personal space.

Brahman

From the Hindu religion, the name of the supreme god.

Causal

All realms of consciousness above the astral.

Center

A state where the ego desires are dormant and a person feels content within his or her own being.

Chakra

Energy interfaces, resembling spinning disks, that convert higher energies into the nervous system of a physical body.

Chi

Vitality, life force energy.

Clairvoyance

Literally means "clear seeing": enhanced vision, the ability to see objects and actions beyond normal perception.

Clearing Work

Self-development work to uncover the core issues that define how a person interacts in the world. *See* ego.

Conditioning

Adaptive patterns of behavior that ensure survival of an organism, but also limit the awareness of reality as it is.

Consciousness

Can be described as awareness of existence and self. Some categorize it into: everyday awareness, sleep, and higher faculties.

Collective Unconscious

Sum of unconscious transpersonal elements of the psyche.

Darshan

Transmission of higher energy with resultant insight and knowing through grace.

DNA

The twin spiral helix of coded information for the patterns of manifestation.

Dhyana

From Buddhism, the higher esoteric meditation phases.

Ego

A pattern of behaviors designed to find separate identity and to ensure physical survival.

Energy

Capacity for force, potential.

Enlightenment

To shed light on; an illuminated or informed state.

Escape Mechanisms

Acts of fantasy or methods to temporarily leave a current situation that one is not ready to confront.

Esoteric

Hidden, veiled wisdom.

Essence

Pure, unblended energy—a fundamental principle.

Etheric

The interface between the physical body and the astral realm.

Fana

The elimination of the lower egoic tendencies.

Fluid

The elemental material of a realm of consciousness.

Focus

(*n.*) The object of concentration; (*v.*) to align the mind into a single point of awareness.

Full Enlightenment

A state where matter and spirit coexist in total awareness.

Functional Ego

An individual operating system with healthy personal boundaries that allow the formation and survival of an identity separate from family and others and acceptable to society.

Glitches

Those aspects in the self that hide undeveloped areas.

Gnosis

A gift of grace that frequently leads to a mystical insight.

Grace

A benevolent transmission of insight, clarity, or focus without any requirement from the recipient.

Grounding

A practice to bring or maintain higher energies into the physical body.

Guru

A person who spans the entire spectrum of consciousness and is able to animate any level in order to teach others.

Healthy Ego

A personal pattern operating in mundane reality with well-established personal boundaries allowing the formation and survival of an identity separate from family and others that acts independently.

Higher Bodies

Vehicles created and used in more evolved, higher vibratory realities. These include the dream body and the diamond body.

Hubris

Arrogance.

Identity

An immovable center, the true self.

Illusion

Anything that is not the truth.

Initiation

An introduction to a higher understanding or awareness.

Invocation

A formal connection to a higher source of energy.

Issues

Points of contention; in spiritual work, this usually refers to ego issues.

Karma

Literally "action" that gives rise to the cause-and-effect relationship.

Koan

A paradoxical puzzle; the solution requires understanding from a higher realm of consciousness.

Kundalini

The goddess responsible for the creation of the higher energy connections to the creation of the physical form. Later, usually at puberty, she rises from her sleeping at the base of the spine to awaken each chakra as she returns up the spine to her divine consort.

Lineage

Direct transmission of a system of knowledge from the source to the present.

Mala

Similar to a rosary or prayer beads. Used as a tool of remembrance and meditation.

Marker

Indication of a significant event, place, or awareness.

Maya

The great illusion of the phenomenal world.

Meditation Map

An established path with universal markers at defined levels of consciousness.

Membrane

A barrier to the next higher realm of consciousness.

Mindfulness

Practice to attain awareness and interconnectedness to all life.

Morphogenic Field

An energetic pattern or blueprint for manifestation.

Mudra

A physical gesture invoked or to invoke psychic energy.

Mystical Oneness

A state of boundless identity with all.

Mystic

A functional mystic is someone who can operate in full realization of the ultimate truths while remaining fully engaged in the mundane world.

Mystical State

A realm of being beyond phenomenal manifestations and yet within which all phenomenal manifestations are brought forth and undergo change.

Mythic Role

An association with a character who has problems similar to ours so that his or her story provides insight in how to deal with common human issues.

Nirvana

"To extinguish"; used to describe the liberated state of consciousness.

Observer Effect

A change in matter when a property is observed.

Ouroboros

The snake who eats his own tail.

Personality Patterns

A combination of qualities, acts, or tendencies.

Prana

The energy of the breath that moves through the subtle pathways of the body-mind.

Pure Land

A Buddhist compassionate realm of consciousness where spiritual progress is ensured to continue.

Purusa

Absolute spirit encompassing a timeless quality with a quiet inner peace.

Qabala

A Judaic school of mysticism.

Realized People

Individuals who not only understand their own unique talents, abilities, and gifts, but also their true role within the world.

Relativity

Einstein's theory that explains gravity as the distortion of space and time together. If space-time is distorted, there must be matter. Einstein also revealed the effect of different perspectives in his theorem of special relativity.

Rita

Underlying order that naturally leads to the establishment of the natural sciences.

Ritual

Conscious repetitious body actions that are based on cosmic structures and/or sacred presences.

Sandpile

A technique to gather and add energies to the individual consciousness in order to form a cohesive group identity.

Satori

Zen version of the mystical state.

Shadow

The socially unacceptable and personally rejected aspects of the psyche.

Shayk

Leader and/or teacher of a Sufi group.

Shock

An impacting event that introduces a reality beyond what a person is conditioned to expect.

Singularity

A point where the laws of physics are invalid. Singularities are predicted to arise inside of black holes at their very centers.

Soul

The permanent culmination of a life's experience that exists beyond physical death.

Spiritual Path

Proven method of self-development that leads to the mystical state.

Sweet Spot

A moving posture that produces a blissful flow of energy to the body while enlightening the mind.

Talmud

A record of two thousand years of oral teachings. An aggregation of law, parable, and philosophy.

Tantra

"To weave." Represents the interwoven male and female cosmic forces.

Taoism

Chinese school of mysticism. Taoism cultivates the wholeness of being with the wholeness of the universe. Based on the *Tao-Te Ching* and the writings of Lao-Tzo and Chuang-Tzo.

Tarot

An esoteric rendition of archetypal principles on the spiritual path depicted on a stylized deck of cards.

Teacher

The capitalized form indicates a being that has mastered his or her own being in order to embody the divine. The teacher is willing to take on the karma of others in order to continue evolving consciousness.

Time-loops

Journeys that loop from present to future and then backward to the present. The origin and ending point may be at the same time and space, but in separate parallel universes.

Tools

Any method, concept, or act that one uses to uncover the true self.

Torah

The sacred mystical text comprised of the five books of Moses.

Triad

The threefold dynamic of consciousness, form, and spirit.

Trinity

Universal symbol for dynamics of separation and the resultant resolution.

True Self

The realized divine aspect of self within.

Upanishads

Hindu teachings, meaning "seated at the feet of the teacher," implying that higher understanding involves an experiential component or energetic transmission from a more highly evolved being.

Vehicle

Body made according to the level of reality in which it is functioning. The physical body operates in three-dimensional reality, the astral or dream body in the world of dreams, and the diamond body in true reality.

Visualization

A meditative journey that allows you, by simple suggestions, to fill in gaps with images from your own consciousness. If used to preoccupy the mind, visualization can lead to higher realms of awareness.

Wave-Particle Duality

Two separate forms of matter that cannot be observed at the same time. Wave properties are distributed throughout space while particles are found in time.

Will

Conscious volition.

Wisdom School

Small esoteric organizations and mystical branches from various religions that maintain a wisdom tradition of evolving higher consciousness for personal and planetary development.

Work

Spiritual work for the evolution of consciousness.

BIBLIOGRAPHY

Campbell, Joseph. *The Hero with a Thousand Faces*. 2nd ed. Princeton, N.J.: Princeton University Press, 1968.

Castaneda, Carlos. *The Art of Dreaming*. New York: Perennial, 1993.

——. *Active Side of Infinity*. New York: Perennial, 2000.

Chittick, William C. *The Sufi Path of Love*. Albany, N.Y.: SUNY Press, 1983.

Corless, Roger J. *The Vision of Buddhism*. New York: Paragon House, 1989.

Danielou, Alain. *The Myths and Gods of India*. Rochester, Vt.: Inner Tradition, 1991.

Darling, David. *Equations of Eternity*. New York: Hyperion, 1993.

Easwaran, Eknath. *Classics of Indian Spirituality*. Berkeley, Calif.: Nilgiri Press, 1987.

Fremantle, Grancesca, and Chogyam Trungpa. *The Tibetan Book of the Dead*. Boston: Shambhala, 1987.

Gawain, Shakti. *Creative Visualization*. New World Library, 2002.

James, William. *The Varieties of Religious Experience*. New York: Collier Books, 1961.

Jaynes, Julian. *The Origin of Consciousness in the Breakdown of the Bicameral Mind*. Boston: Houghton Mifflin, 1976.

Judith, Anodea. *Wheels of Life*. St. Paul, Minn.: Llewellyn Publications, 1995.

Killer, John M. *The Indian Way*. New York: Macmillan Publishing, 1982.

Krishnamurti, Jiddu. *Freedom from the Known*. San Francisco: Harper-SanFrancisco, 1975.

———. *Meeting Life*. San Francisco: HarperSanFrancisco, 1991.

McGraw, Phil. *Self Matters*. New York: Simon & Shuster, 2001.

Mitchell, Stephen. *Tao Te Ching*. San Francisco: HarperCollins, 1994.

———. *The Gospel According to Jesus*. San Francisco: HarperCollins, 1991.

Ni, Hua-Ching. *The Taoist Inner View of the Universe and the Immortal Realm*. The Shrine of the Eternal Breath of Tao. Malibu, Calif.: 1979.

Ornstein, Robert. *Evolution of Consciousness*. New York: Simon & Shuster, 1991.

Pagels, Elaine. *The Gnostic Gospels*. New York: Vintage Books, 1979.

Russel, Peter. *The Global Brain Awakens*. Palo Alto, Calif.: Global Brain Inc., 1995.

Schimmel, Annemarie. *Mystical Dimensions of Islam*. Chapel Hill, N.C.: University of North Carolina Press, 1975.

Sheldrake, Rupert. *A New Science of Life*. Rochester, Vt.: Inner Traditions, 1981.

Smith, Huston. *The World's Religions*. San Francisco: HarperSanFrancisco, 1998.

Wangyal, Tenzin. *The Tibetan Yogas of Dream and Sleep*. Ithaca, N.Y.: Snow Lion Publications, 1998.

Wilson, Colin. *The Essential Colin Wilson*. Berkeley, Calif.: Celestial Arts, 1986.

Wolf, Fred Alan. *Taking the Quantum Leap*. New York: Harper & Row, 1989.

INDEX

☽ ORDER LLEWELLYN BOOKS TODAY!

Llewellyn publishes hundreds of books on your favorite subjects! To get these exciting books, including the ones on the following pages, check your local bookstore or order them directly from Llewellyn.

Order Online:

Visit our website at www.llewellyn.com, select your books, and order them on our secure server.

Order by Phone:

- Call toll-free within the U.S. at 1-877-NEW-WRLD (1-877-639-9753)
  Call toll-free within Canada at 1-866-NEW-WRLD (1-866-639-9753)
- We accept VISA, MasterCard, and American Express

Order by Mail:

Send the full price of your order (MN residents add 7% sales tax) in U.S. funds, plus postage & handling to:

> **Llewellyn Worldwide**
> **P.O. Box 64383, Dept. 0-7387-0502-0**
> **St. Paul, MN 55164-0383, U.S.A.**

Postage & Handling:

Standard (U.S., Mexico, & Canada). If your order is:
> Up to $25.00, add $3.50
> $25.01 - $48.99, add $4.00
> $49.00 and over, FREE STANDARD SHIPPING

(Continental U.S. orders ship UPS. AK, HI, PR, & P.O. Boxes ship USPS 1st class. Mex. & Can. ship PMB.)

International Orders:

Surface Mail: For orders of $20.00 or less, add $5 plus $1 per item ordered. For orders of $20.01 and over, add $6 plus $1 per item ordered.

Air Mail:
Books: Postage & Handling is equal to the total retail price of all books in the order.
Non-book items: Add $5 for each item.

Orders are processed within 2 business days. Please allow for normal shipping time.
Postage and handling rates subject to change.

Meditation for Beginners
Techniques for Awareness, Mindfulness & Relaxation

STEPHANIE JEAN CLEMENT, PH.D.

Perhaps the greatest boundary we set for ourselves is the one between the conscious and less conscious parts of our own minds. We all need a way to gain deeper understanding of what goes on inside our minds when we are awake, asleep, or just not paying attention. Meditation is one way to pay attention long enough to find out.

Meditation for Beginners offers a step-by-step approach to meditation, with exercises that introduce you to the rich possibilities of this age-old spiritual practice. Improve concentration, relax your body quickly and easily, work with your natural healing ability, and enhance performance in sports and other activities. Just a few minutes each day is all that's needed.

- Contains step-by-step meditation exercises

- Shows how to develop a consistent meditation effort in just a few minutes each day

- Explores many different ways to meditate, including kundalini yoga, walking meditation, dream meditation, tarot meditations, healing meditation

ISBN 0-7387-0203-X, 264 pp., 5¾₆ x 8 $12.95
Also available in Spanish

Illuminations
The Healing of the Soul

DOLORES ASHCROFT-NOWICKI

Even the most enlightened seekers can experience the Dark Night of the Soul: feelings of spiritual desolation, loneliness, and hopelessness. Now renowned author and mystic Dolores Ashcroft-Nowicki shares a magical healing process she discovered during her own "dark night," a system based on the mystical energies of the Hebrew letters.

It is a twenty-two-step program of self-growth and spiritual healing based on the twenty-two ancient symbols of the Hebrew alphabet. Through prayer, meditation (pathworking), and ritual work, the energies of the Hebrew letters can provide the strength, wisdom, and creative power of an infinitely compassionate source.

- Written by a widely respected esoteric teacher and author

- The first book to use the magical powers of the entire Hebrew alphabet to alleviate spiritual suffering and achieve breakthroughs in self-awareness

- Provides prayers that speak to the divine intelligence within each letter

- Explores the numerology, images, and associated meanings of each letter in depth

- Contains twenty-two original pathworkings and rituals

ISBN 0-7387-0186-6, 360 pp., 7½ x 9⅛ $19.95

To order, call 1-877-NEW-WRLD
Prices subject to change without notice

10 Steps to a Magical Life
Meditations and Affirmations for Personal Growth and Happiness

ADRIAN CALABRESE

For a decade, Adrian Calabrese has helped others to unleash their spiritual power to achieve their greatest potential and create miracles in their lives. Now she outlines her simple approach that exceeds any religious dogma and offers the opportunity for unlimited spiritual growth.

You will learn how to tap into your extraordinary divine power to create a joyful, abundant life. When you follow the steps faithfully, you will begin to see your life change in a very special way. Not only will you become happier and more sensitive to others, you will notice that you suddenly attract whatever your heart desires!

- Organized into ten simple steps that will awaken your magical, mystical and hidden powers

- Each chapter ends with an affirmation or declarative statement of prayer

- Inspires readers of all ages, religions and belief systems to examine their own situations and follow their unique path of self-discovery and inner awareness

- Reveals a simple practice that will transform even the most mundane task into a magical event

ISBN 0-7387-0311-7, 240 pp., 6 x 9 $14.95

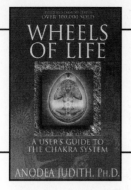

Wheels of Life

A User's Guide to the Chakra System

ANODEA JUDITH

As portals between the physical and spiritual planes, chakras represent the sacred architecture of your body and psyche. This classic introduction to the chakras, which has sold over 100,000 copies, has been completely updated and expanded. In addition to revised chapters on relationships, evolution, and healing, it includes a new section on raising children with healthy chakras.

Wheels of Life takes you on a wondrous journey through the progressively transcendent levels of consciousness. View this ancient metaphysical system by the light of new metaphors such as body work and quantum physics. Learn how to explore your own chakras using poetic meditations, physical expression, and visionary art.

ISBN 0-87542-320-5, 480 pp., 6 x 9 $17.95